BRIDGING THE GAP

For those who asked
and for Jack O'Connor
'God's man in Salthill'
in the 1990s

Joseph Pollard

Bridging the Gap

CONNECTING WITH
QUESTIONING CATHOLICS

First published in 2001 by
the columba press
55A Spruce Avenue, Stillorgan Industrial Park,
Blackrock, Co Dublin

Cover by Bill Bolger
Origination by The Columba Press
Printed in Ireland by Colour Books Ltd, Dublin

ISBN 1 85607 326 2

Acknowledgements
Scripture quotations are taken from *The New Revised Standard Version,* copyright © 1989, by the Division of Christian Education of the National Council of the Churches of Christ in the United States of America.

Contents

Abbreviations

Old Testament
Gen (Genesis)
Ex (Exodus)
1 Chr (Chronicles)
Ps (Psalms)
Jer (Jeremiah)
Hos (Hosea)

New Testament
Mt (Matthew)
Mk (Mark)
Lk (Luke)
Jn (John)
Acts (Acts of the Apostles)
Rom (Romans)
1 Cor (1st Corinthians)
2 Cor (2nd Corinthians)
Gal (Galatians)
Ephes (Ephesians)
Col (Colossians)
1 Tim (1st Timothy)
Heb (Hebrews)
1 Pt (1st Peter)
2 Pt (2nd Peter)
1 Jn (1st John)
Rev (Revelation)

Introduction

The final decade of the century did not end in a rush of glory for the church. It was a painful decade. It seemed that the revelation of child abuse scandals would never end. It was painful to watch the initial inaction of the church authorities and the late responses that satisfied few people. The church was perplexed.

Many people saw not only a too human side of the church but also an incompetent one. The young and the middle-aged questioned the divine origin of the church and many wondered about its right to educate and nurture anyone. At least one public figure stated bluntly that children should be kept far away from the clergy.

It was a decade of disappearances. Large numbers abandoned the church, its rituals and the 1600-year-old tradition that had endured so much throughout its Irish history and which one hoped would finish the second millennium with a flourish. The hierarchy received dismissive treatment in the media, vocations dwindled, religious pulled out of schools, seminaries were sold or found a different purpose for their buildings, convents became hotels and a few rural communities woke up one day and found that they were on the cutting-edge of the new religious world – their local church no longer had a priest.

It was a decade of alternatives. On the heels of the disappearing Catholic ethos came more alternative schools, ideologies, religions, concerns, agendas, values, mentalities and lifestyles. The 1990s presented a huge challenge to the church since it was the church's departing members that were the flesh and blood of these new alternatives. The whole process of Catholic contraction, on the one hand, and alternative expansion, on the other, was in the pipeline long before the 1990s of course, and one could argue over its causes and its inevitability. Nonetheless, the church seemed to be so perplexed with its own internal condition that it became a church of silence in the face of this other pastoral phenomenon. It had a major fight on its hands and it did not even bother, so it appeared, to enter the ring.

Against this backdrop, it was disappointing to see the church settle mainly for statues and sundry markers for Jubilee 2000 when it did not also undertake a massive countrywide programme of open pastoral fora, adult religious dialogue and a new evangelisation in response to the obvious signs of the times in Irish society.

This book will not redeem the 1990s; it is not intended that it should even try. Nor is it God's model for a new inter-generational dialogue, nor does it speak for the 'official' church. In the minds of young and old any priest is official enough and I happened to be – willingly – in their line of fire. It is a modest response to those I met up with on our mutual pilgrim way during the last years of that decade. It comes out of the place where priest and people cross each other's lives day by day, far from officialdom, and find that they are travelling the same road of faith with the same questions and concerns and living out of an increasing reliance on the Lord alone.

Questions first came my way in scripture classes. These were from the older generation mainly. Then they came from the university-educated generation of family members, their friends and acquaintances. It is not hard to spot the concerns of the two groups. The younger group are now in their late twenties and early thirties and are about to become the pivotal Irish generation in terms of social leadership and the church's future. The questions are a sample of what bothers them about their church. I find that they are honest young people who are very open to the church anytime it wishes to engage honestly and openly with them. Connections are still there to be made.

The Catholic Church in Ireland may be at its most critical point since the Reformation. The younger generation's disillusionment with it comes at a time when education, democracy, the questioning spirit, self-determination, job availability and the independence of money combine to challenge the church in terms of both the mind and the heart. It simply must become a pro-active church in a manner unknown to it in the past. This book is only a word in that process.

I have collated the questions and framed the wording that best expresses them. I think I do the questions justice. Whether my responses do them justice is another matter. You are the judge of that. What I write is one older believer's response to the questions and the hurts, the shyness and the silence. I hope my responses are dialogical and a step in the right pastoral direction.

How could they? Priests and children

The face of Brendan Smyth is Ireland's image of perversity. It is the face we saw in the media – growling, leering, seemingly unrepentant and defiant. We named him a monster, a beast, an obscenity, a demon out of hell. Other versions of Brendan Smyth followed. The swimming coaches. The orphanages. The Magdalen laundries. The industrial schools. Some of these were probably worse because they combined sexual and physical abuse, and the crimes occurred in official institutions and in a controlled environment.

How could priests (and religious brothers and nuns) do such shocking things? There is perversity in any adult who sexually abuses a child. There is an additional gospel perversity in an ordained 'man of God' like Smyth abusing an innocent 'child of God'. The gospel of Mark has this poignant incident and it is one of the most tender scenes in scripture:

> People were bringing little children to him in order that he might touch them; and the disciples spoke sternly to them. But when Jesus saw this, he was indignant and said to them, 'Let the little children come to me; do not stop them; for it is to such as these that the kingdom of God belongs.' ... And he took them up in his arms, laid his hands on them, and blessed them.
> (Mk 10:13-16)

For a Christian, there cannot be a worse child abuser than a priest because of this gospel image of Jesus with the children, and because of the obvious contradiction between what ought to be and what is. In addition, parents and adults feel psychologically at sea when their leaders and role models become the predators of their children. By religion and by instinct of nature, we are shaken to our foundations.

So, we banish the child predators from our midst. The easiest way to banish them is to name them beasts or demons from hell. But they are not. To name them inhuman is to help them evade their responsibility and our own.

Child abusers are as old as the human race. Some cultures do not even frown on them. I know of no society devoid of child sexual abuse irrespective of civil law and religious taboo. The roots of abuse are deeper than law and taboo. To medical people, they are in the psyche. That is true. But theology roots abuse even deeper. The abusive tendency is part of our awfully flawed nature that resulted from original sin.

In the western world the phenomenon of child sexual abuse first became public in the United States. Over here, we were smug about it. America is a pagan place, we said, and such perversity could not happen in Catholic Ireland! Had we forgotten that flawed human nature is the same all over the world?

As much as 20% of the US population may be victims of sexual abuse, with most of this occurring in childhood and teen years. Is this indicative of the percentage in other countries, including our own? The prominent media cases, of course, involve clergy, educators, medical personnel and celebrities. Truck drivers and plumbers are less saleable to the media as child abusers. However, various studies show that the incidence of child sexual abuse is highest in family life, not in the professions. This shocks people. Yet we should expect it for rather obvious reasons: most predators are found in family life, where most men are, and most children are reared in the institution of the home, a highly controlled environment against which the child has no easy appeal.

Why are men (women, to a far lesser degree) child sexual abusers? Psychologists point to the sexual dynamics and psyche of the male and to his arrested sexual development. A child abuser is a psychologically undeveloped person, woefully lacking in appropriate adult relationships and social responsibility. Since the priesthood is composed of men it would be remarkable not to find any abusers in it.

A by-product of the child sexual abuse revelations is the questioning for the first time by some Catholics of the seminary system and even of the celibate requirement for priesthood. On the face of it, is not the seminary a natural attraction for paedophiles? And is not the celibate nature of a man an added push toward covert sexual expression in some form? And is not the traditional interaction of the celibate priest with children in the setting of school, catechism, playground, Mass serving, sacramental preparation, etc., a real danger to both of them? I do not have easy answers. Does anyone? I can say from personal experience, at any rate, that celibacy vis-à-vis children is not of itself a liability. Nor does it seem to be for unmarried adults in other professions who have a great deal of interaction with children, e.g. doctors and teachers and counsellors. The child sexual abuser's psychological profile is quite distinct from the celibate or married person. One does not sexually abuse a child on the basis of being married or single or celibate or heterosexual or homosexual. Even children sexually abuse other children.

It should not surprise us that latent child abusers enter seminaries in response to what they perceive as a call to priesthood. They enter all the professions and none. They enter the married state. It should not surprise us that paedophiles who entered seminaries in the past were easily ordained. For one thing, they were not identifiable as monsters or demons from hell. They could be intelligent, sensitive and gentle men. At any rate, their sexual tendencies were hidden and had no scope in childless seminaries. The seminary had no psychological screening of candidates as we know it today. Seminaries relied for the selection of men for priestly ordination on general assessments of a man's suitability for priesthood rather than on true psychological evaluations and standards. Such were not available in the past. They are today. While they do not identify the latent paedophile as such, a candidate's deficiency in psycho-sexual development will put him among those in need of on-going counselling and evaluation.

One observer (Donal Dorr in *The Furrow*, Oct 2000) suggests that clerical child abuse may be due not only to paedophilia as such but to the kind of sexual morality taught in seminaries and to Catholics in the past. In this morality, all sexual sin was mortal, even a 'bad thought'. Could such an accounting of every sexual sin as fully mortal have contributed to an insensitivity in regard to the seriousness of child sexual abuse and to the guilt and shame that victims so easily and so wrongly felt in themselves? All was far from well in the church's moral theology of that time.

None of these considerations, of course, takes away the anger and the hurt that people have over the past behaviour of bishops who swept these things under the carpet. By merely moving the offenders from assignment to assignment they continued the cycle of abuse and increased the number of victims. It may help people a little to know that bishops have now apologised for their clergy's abuse and thereby, at least implicitly, for their own inactivity about it in the past. From my own experience of the past, I know that many bishops were confused by the whole phenomenon and were at a loss in knowing what to do. I served as theologian to a genuinely holy archbishop who had great difficulty being convinced that a young, popular priest of his was an abuser of children. I confronted another bishop at a convocation of clergy because he supported a public apology from the priests but wanted himself and his brother bishops excluded from the apology.

I believe that all priests were taken aback when the first child abuse cases began to surface. As an example, I had gone through six years of seminary formation, six years of parish ministry, three years of post-graduate studies in Rome, and some years in diocesan administration and had never met a child-abusing priest or knew of one. My priest friends and I never talked of the matter because it was an unknown quantity among us. No parishioner ever mentioned an abusing priest or religious brother or nun to me. And I had plenty of lay friends who found me easy to talk to. It is for these reasons that I am able to understand why the bishops were unprepared for the number of the child abuse cases that came to light. Nonetheless, when they did come to light the bishops handled the issue, the perpetrators, the victims and their families in a way that people felt was inexcusable.

Today we are becoming aware of the other side of the coin. There are innocent priests in every country who are accused falsely of child sexual abuse. They, too, are victims. They are not presumed innocent until proven guilty. They are immediately suspended from ministry. The argument here is that the temper of the times demands such action and that church authorities must be seen to be meticulously the reverse of what they were in the past. The assumption then is that once an investigation has been completed favourably, these men will resume their ministry.

It is not only the temper of the times but also, according to some critics, the fear of the financial bankruptcy of dioceses that accounts for this present-day abandonment of a priest's basic human right. Very often there is no due process worthy of the name in the church nor is there a resolution of the charge against the priest unless he himself initiates a civil law action. Even if an accused priest is exonerated in time, he and his family are tainted for life. We end up with priests distrusting their bishops and many of them refusing anything but a bare-bones pastoral ministry to children. Children have, ironically, become a pastoral problematic for priests. It's all a long way from the image of Jesus putting his arms around the little children.

What of the future? All the revelations and criticisms and anger have had a good effect across the board in the church, in civil society, and in the institutions and the professions. We can be sure of a number of things. Predatory adults can never again assume the silence of their child victims. Children need not despair anymore of their accusations being met automatically with the disbelief of parents, clergy, teachers, social workers and police. Parents and guardians will become more protective of their children, and better educated themselves in the telltale signs. The public will face up to the most critical side of the whole question: the prevalence of child sexual abuse in the home. And all of us have to face the sobering truth that the sexual abuse of children has a long history and may not disappear in this or any foreseeable generation.

As for the church, there is already a seismic shift in attitude and action in some countries, especially the US. Something has happened there already that would normally require generations for the slow machinery of the church to achieve. The American bishops persuaded Rome to change church law in line with how seriously American civil law regards child sexual abuse. As a consequence, a priest can suffer grave penalties including laicisation (i.e. being stripped of priesthood and returned to the lay state). In addition, the sexual abuse of anyone up to the age of 18 (it was 16) is now considered to be child sexual abuse. This may be an extreme age parameter given the sexual mores of young people in our western culture but, at least, it shows the determination of the bishops.

Critics note that these changes by the church came only after the change in civil law and possibly as its consequence. And they argue rather cynically that the changes are due to the financial ruin of a number of smaller US dioceses and the near-bankruptcy of others which occurred from sexual abuse cases that were lost in the courts, and to the sheer embarrassment of the church and its bishops, and to the public outcry against the church. But that's neither here nor there in human terms. The point is: the children win.

How can they? Homosexual clergy

I think that if a known homosexual priest were appointed PP of a parish there would be a 'disturbance'. We may be more aware of the sexual realities of life today than we were in the past and our tolerance of 'odd' lifestyles may be quite expansive for such as rockers and artists and celebrities, but we have our limits.

The disturbance might be transparent enough in rural parishes but more subtle in sophisticated urban settings. In both cases it would be equally unfortunate.

I've always felt that people are tolerant and draw lines in the sand only when what is absolutely crucial to them – their marriage or their children or their worldview – is threatened. Homosexuality appears to many people to threaten their marriage, or the institution of marriage, their children, and their understanding of God's order in life.

The fact is that there are many homosexual parish priests and curates and bishops throughout the world and they seem to be doing just as well pastorally as all the other parish priests and curates and bishops who are heterosexual.

When you say things like that, some people raise their eyes to heaven, or call you a liberal, or feel that you are probably 'one of them'. Others blame your sad state on Vatican II and the insanity they feel it unleashed. But in a classroom setting or in a discussion group, someone will cut through the fog of emotion, face the issue, and simply ask why we never heard of a homosexual parish priest in the old days. There is an answer.

Although there was never a church law against it, a known homosexual priest would not be made a PP in the old days and, similarly, a known homosexual student would be quietly steered out of the seminary. It would be done without fuss or animosity, just following custom. It would be done from ignorance of the nature of the homosexual orientation, from a sense of decorum, and from a confusion of the homosexual condition with that of the child sexual abuser. Nonetheless, homosexuals did survive the seminary programme, were ordained, and became parish priests. I suspect that many people in the parishes are still unclear on the nature of homosexuality and do not realise that it is not a barrier to priesthood and promotion in the church.

It is hard to blame them. They always heard that homosexuality was wrong. I recall that, in as short a space of time as ten or twelve years, American psychiatry described homosexuality as a sexual dysfunction, then as a condition without definite medical pathology, then as a pathology, and finally as an acceptable lifestyle. Critics at the time felt that this was a cave-in to pressure from the civil rights movement. The post-Vatican II church relies on the input of the behavioural sciences when making its ethical evaluations of human behaviour, and for arriving at its moral judgements, and when issuing its pastoral guidelines to the clergy and the people. Obviously, it is hard to do all this when the medical expertise relied upon changes so much.

The homosexual condition is called a 'disorder' by the official church today. But the church does not describe this homosexual condition as something the homosexual is personally responsible for. It is homosexual activity, or the acting out of this condition, or being a 'practising' homosexual that is considered sinful, and such activity is a bar to seminary life and to ordination. This is the heart of the matter in terms of answering the question, 'How can the church ordain homosexuals and how can we have homosexual priests running our parishes?'

Would a practising homosexual parish priest be acceptable to the church? The answer is no. A practising heterosexual parish priest is not acceptable either. The same norms of sexual abstinence apply to both. The condition of being homosexual, then, is not the issue: homosexual activity is.

There is no reason why a chaste homosexual should not be as gifted and as pastoral a parish priest as anyone else. And there is no evidence to support parents' fear that their children are at greater risk if their priest is homosexual. The homosexual condition is not the condition of the child sexual abuser and the sexual drive is neither more nor less intense in the homosexual person than it is in anyone else.

Some readers who are heterosexual may be surprised at this apparent leniency of the church towards homosexuals. On the other hand, readers who are homosexual may see it as nothing more than moral minimalism. They are not happy with this minimalism at all. The current discussion on the church and homosexuals has moved far beyond the question of appointing parish priests who are non-practising homosexuals. The current issues have to do with whether there must be a place in the church for practising homosexuals, whether there should be an acceptance of permanent homosexual partnerships, and why the church's understanding of homosexual rights lags so far behind that of secular society.

At the present time, the official church is at odds with western culture on these questions. The church does not countenance the homosexual lifestyle. It has no provision for homosexual 'marriages' or for the blessing of exclusive homosexual partnerships which Christian counsellors may encourage in preference to hanging loose and playing the field. The church keeps within the limits of scripture as it understands it. The only kind of marriage championed in the bible is that of man and woman. And while there is a contemporary debate among scholars over the biblical texts that appear to condemn homosexuality, the church insists that sexual activity must be expressed only within the traditional married state.

This presents severe difficulties for Catholics who are 'true' homosexuals. Many believe that their sexual orientation is not a matter of psychological disorder or of personal choice but of constitution. They are born that way. To them it is a natural thing. It is, as one writer puts it, 'a fact of creation'.[1] If, as Catholic theology says, one's sexuality is a gift from God then the homosexual's sexuality is as much God's gift as the sexuality of heterosexual persons. In their case, homosexuals say, there's no point in suggesting some form of intensive counselling or of reparative therapy; nor is it fair to insist that they commit themselves to a life of celibacy which they would not freely choose in any event.

The church's pastoral responses to homosexuals' concerns are, as they see them, inadequate as far as the 'true' or 'born that way' homosexuals are concerned. The responses all presuppose that the homosexual condition is a disorder in nature and not a gift. They assume that most homosexuals can be changed by therapy and that those who can't must, with God's grace, commit themselves to the single, chaste life. The church does not accept the homosexual lifestyle as an equal or alternative way of life for a believer. This seems to me to be the point of departure between the church and western society in general on the question of homosexual rights.

Hence, there is a general antipathy among homosexuals towards their church and there is a general writing-off of the church by counsellors who see the church as counter-productive to their efforts with gay men and women.

But to return to our main focus in this essay and to a question raised in clergy circles all the time: Are there more homosexuals in the seminaries today than in the past? The answer is debatable because while we have some data on homosexual percentages in seminaries today, no such data is available for the past. Homosexuals did not willingly reveal themselves in the past, except perhaps to their spiritual directors, and so there is no way of knowing. For the same reason, we do not know what percentage of the general public was homosexual in the past. Even current statistics are unreliable and the figure given for one country, the US, ranges from 5% to 14%. Those of us who have taught in seminaries recently feel that the percentage in priestly formation is higher than heretofore, but we would question whether this is disproportionately higher than what obtains in society at large.

There is a fear among some priests and people that too many homosexuals in the priesthood, even if they are perfectly chaste, would be a bad thing for the future of parishes. But it seems a difficult matter to me how one would decide what the ideal proportion is. A percentage that mirrors one's own society or nation might be a normal expectation.

There is also a fear in priests and people that the pastoral relationship between priest and parishioner would be impacted negatively if there were too many homosexual clergy. I do not know. But I realise that, taking even the lowest figure of 5% of the population as homosexual, tens of thousands of homosexual priests must have served the people in the parishes over the past two millennia. One assumes from the silence of the historical records that they did a good job. One may also assume that many of them were saints.

How could they? The banished babies

There is a *lios* behind my house. The first time I saw it from my back window I was delighted; delighted in the way a painter or an archaeologist or a returned exile would be. It is a large hill with great steps that are carved at intervals and that run the entire width of the hill from east to west, all covered in a carpet of green. Dozens of white sheep graze the steps, above and below each other, in military formations.

What is underneath? Bronze-age earthworks? The temple of a pagan god bested by Patrick? A chieftain's fort? Or is it one of those sad places where generations of broken-hearted Irish parents brought their unbaptised babies for burial, their pain doubled by their church's banishment of them to unconsecrated ground? I do not know and, down deep, maybe I don't want to know. But I suppose I'll have to face the truth even if it clouds my view and disturbs my peace. If I find it's a place of banishment I'll still look out my back window because it's March now and the sheep have their new lambs. And I will not pray for the children: I'll pray to them. Surely we should know where all such banished babies are? Surely they are with the Lamb of God.

Do I have someone in such a place? Did my mother miscarry late? Did a 'flu or a fever carry off a sibling between birth and the baptismal font? And is this something that has been hidden from me for all of my sixty-four years?

Strange as it may seem, I had never heard of this practice until I watched a program about it on TV. I had not even heard of it in the seminary despite being surrounded by students from nearly every county in the land. Pastoral customs were taught to us in the seminary but there was no mention of this one. Our theology classes covered the burial rites for infants but there was no hint of this phenomenon.

Church law also dealt with death and burial. It mentioned the believer's right to a Christian burial in consecrated ground. Consecrated ground is appropriate as the resting place of a body that awaits its future resurrection. It is appropriate for a funeral ritual that sprinkles the body with holy water and perfumes it with incense. It seemed logical enough then that the church would exclude from consecrated ground the really big and unrepentant public sinner. Suicides were also excluded. This was based on the common assumption of the day that theirs was a calculated act of self-destruction and a denial of trust in providence. A true child of God would never act that way. We know better, of course, today.

But why the banished babies? I'll begin by speaking for myself and saying that I find the church's exclusion of these infants regrettable. It must have been heart-breaking especially for mothers. Now I'll try to understand the thinking behind it and where it might have come from.

When we were small there was a church teaching called limbo. I can even remember the definition of it from the old school catechism. Limbo was a place in the next life for those babies of Christian parents who died before they could be baptised. Jesus said: 'No one can enter the kingdom of God without being born of water and Spirit.' (Jn 3:5) For the church, baptism is paramount. And these babies were not baptised. So the church reasoned as follows: These children cannot enter heaven and therefore should not be buried in consecrated ground. That ground is reserved for those awaiting the resurrection. These babies died while still stained with original sin. On the other hand, they are innocent of any personal sin. What is their destiny? It isn't heaven and it cannot be hell. And it cannot be purgatory because purgatory is a place for those who have a 'debt' of punishment owing on their personal sins. Infants have no such 'debt' because they have no personal sins. So, with heaven, hell and purgatory excluded for unbaptised infants, the early church came up with the idea of limbo, a form of natural blessedness.

Limbo is not a medieval invention as some critics in and outside the church say. It was the early church's response to Christian parents who lost babies in goodly numbers to persecution and high infant mortality rates. These were parents who intended to baptise their infants but did not get the chance to do so. Limbo was intended as a consolation for them. It is a sort of Christian version of *sheol,* the resting place of the Hebrew patriarchs, the place that Jesus visited between his death and his resurrection. We refer to *sheol* every Sunday at Mass during the creed when we affirm: 'He descended into hell.' This not the hell of the damned, as we learned in the old catechism, but *sheol.*

Limbo is not mentioned in the authoritative new *Catechism of the Catholic Church.* Instead, the new burial rite for unbaptised infants invites us to trust in God's mercy and to pray for their salvation.

What I have just written may explain the thinking behind the church's view on consecrated ground, on who should be in it, and why unbaptised babies were excluded. For myself as a Christian, there are more important theologies than this one about consecrated ground and unconsecrated ground. Besides, the matter of location doesn't really count in the long run because the resurrection is neither in this place nor in that place: it is in Christ. 'I am the resurrection,' Jesus said. (Jn 11:25)

Faced with their dilemma, Irish parents of unbaptised children sought their own solution. Some went to closed burial grounds among ancient church ruins in the middle of a field or on the side of a hill. I do not know – but I can guess – why others took their unbaptised infants to a *lios* or a rath, to a site associated with fairies or to a site that, long before the fairies, was some pagan burial ground; a place that they knew by instinct and emotion tied them to their ancestors when mother church was absent from their pain and even the cause of it. Blood is thicker than theology and racial memory outdistances the span of Christianity.

My own experience with infant burials has been in America. The baptised and the unbaptised alike were buried in Catholic cemeteries if the family had a plot there. The ground was already consecrated and no blessing was needed for the gravesite. In public cemeteries – unconsecrated ground – you blessed the grave for the unbaptised as you did for the baptised and offered the same commendation prayers equally, and you did your best to comfort the distraught parents equally.

Times change. The Irish church now holds services for the banished babies in these pagan places. This is a public acknowledgement that wrong was done to broken-hearted parents and I suppose it is a sort of apology. Lots of apologies are forthcoming these days from the church, from governments, regimes and sundry agents of yesterday's public and private pain. It may not be enough for the living. It is too late for the dead. The past is not redeemed no matter the prayer, the poetry or the apology. That is one reason why the church needs much more sensitivity and foresight in all matters of the human heart.

As regards the infants who die unbaptised, we read the following in the new *Catechism of the Catholic Church:* 'The church can only entrust them to the mercy of God, as she does in her funeral rites for them. Indeed, the great mercy of God who desires that all men should be saved, and Jesus' tenderness toward children which caused him to say: "Let the children come to me, do not hinder them," allow us to hope that there is a way of salvation for children who have died without baptism.'

What is new here? Well, there is no mention of limbo. And there is no theology of the old legalistic God with a minimalist nature to him. The teaching is still restrictive and will not fully satisfy those who live out of their hearts. Yet the last line is something the church never said in the past. 'Jesus' tenderness allows us to hope that there is a way of salvation for children who have died without baptism.'[2] If the church had said this in time, the phenomenon of the banished babies would never have happened. Some day the church may say even more.

How can they? Annulments

Some people are incensed that the church grants marriage annulments. It seems like a great cave-in to a fickle generation.

Thousands are spent on staging these lavish weddings. Thousands more are spent on gifts. Eloquent wedding ceremonies are scripted to enhance the official rite of the church. The church building itself should be ornate, or sited by the sea, or allowing of the green hills to come in through the windows, or else it will find itself overcome with floral arrangements. The number of priest celebrants is not necessarily a measure of the couple's spiritual depth. It can be a ploy by the mammy to make everyone sit up and take notice. One, two or three bands cater to the different generations and tastes. Spirits flow abundantly and no one has ever been heard to say at an Irish wedding, 'They have no more wine.' (Jn 2:3) A thousand well-wishes and a thousand toasts (over the course of the day and the night) speed the happy couple on their honeymoon.

Five years later you see her (it usually is) waiting for you after Mass. 'I want an annulment. Will you get it for me?' It is not a question. It is an expectation.

What bothers people about annulments are the stern words of Jesus with which they are familiar:

> Some Pharisees … asked, 'Is it lawful for a man to divorce his wife for any cause?' He answered: 'Have you not read that the one who made them at the beginning "made them male and female," and said, "For this reason a man shall leave his father and mother and be joined to his wife, and the two shall become one flesh"? So they are no longer two, but one flesh. Therefore what God has joined together, let no one separate.' (Mt 19: 3-6)

In the next few lines, the Pharisees push Jesus for some exceptions allowing of divorce, but he remains firm with one exception.

The only ground for divorce is adultery (translated 'fornication' in some versions of the bible).

In making this one exception Jesus is not inventing something new but repeating an exception allowed in Judaism. What is this adultery or fornication? What did it mean in Jesus' time? Briefly, there were two schools of opinion in the Lord's time. One said it is sexual intercourse by a married woman with a man not her husband. The other said it is anything 'indecent' from extra-marital intercourse to being a poor cook. Jesus appears to favour the first – and more restrictive – meaning.

But that is not the end of it. The words of Jesus as given in Mark (10:11-12) and Luke (16:18) are different. They record Jesus prohibiting divorce for any reason. Are they more faithful to the exact words of Jesus? Probably. For one thing, Mark's is the oldest version of the gospel. For another, we look at the re-action of the apostles to the words of Jesus. It is the re-action of men who realise that Jesus is challenging them to uphold an ideal of marriage that is permanent and exclusive. They say, in effect, that if things be that way it is better not to risk marriage at all. 'His disciples said to him, "If such is the case of a man with his wife, it is better not to marry".' (Mt 19:10)

People have heard these words over the years, and heard many sermons condemning divorce. Therefore, the current recourse to annulment, and what they see as the easy access to annulments, understandably disturbs them.

Is Jesus trying to hold people to an *ideal* of marriage when he, apparently, makes no allowance for divorce, or is he stating that the ideal must be the *reality* in every single instance? Bible scholars usually stress the ideal. The church stresses the reality in every instance.

In the bible, marriage is a covenanted relationship. It has the same qualities for man and wife as has the covenant between God and God's people. The covenant is more than a contract: it is a consecration. It is permanent. It is exclusive. No other god may come between God and his people in their covenant; no other human may come between this man and his wife in their covenant. That is what Jesus meant when he said, 'What, then, God has joined together; let no man separate.' In the bible, God gives the graces necessary for his people to remain faithful in their covenant with him;

the married couple are similarly graced to preserve their covenant with each other. Scholars and church agree on this biblical theology of Christian marriage as covenanted love. They separate on what to do when a marriage actually breaks down and there is, as the saying goes, no hope of saving it.

In that instance, scholars generally accept the possibility of divorce. For them, the ideal cannot be realised in this instance, maybe for an unpredictable reason. Every possible spiritual, medical and psychological effort should be made, of course, to help the couple prior to a divorce.

If these efforts fail, then divorce is possible on the grounds of Christian understanding, compassion and love. Ecclesiastical rigidity and legalism must not be allowed to stand in the way.

The church, of course, allows no exception to the ideal. So it does not grant divorces. It grants annulments. An annulment is cynically criticised as the Catholic version of divorce. An annulment is a declaration that a 'proper' marriage never existed in the first place. How is this determined? A covenant or a contract is not valid if one of the parties enters it on the basis of coercion or fear. These words are technical terms in church law. They have to do with the quality of the consent given by bride and groom when they said 'I do'. The consent is defective, and the marriage subject to annulment, if the consent is not free. An example of this in the past was undue pressure by the families on the couple to get married. This pressure was sometimes tied to parental concerns about name, inheritance, money and land. Today, defective consent covers a wider range involving personality and psychological maturity. One of the parties might suffer from a serious disorder that was either deliberately hidden or unknown previously to the other party, e.g. abuse, addiction, cruelty. Then again, some people are too immature to understand or live up to the obligations of married life and cannot give a free or 'proper' consent even when they say 'I do'.

I think that a lot of the criticism of annulments arises from the perception that too many are granted; that psychology is an inexact science; that the psychological grounds are too easily stretched; that the whole process chips away at the ideal of marriage; and that those who have stood firm in their marriages, often at great sacrifice, are somehow lessened.

It is commonly believed that annulments are hard to get for ordinary folk but readily available to the rich and famous. I suspect that some royals and rich have received preferential treatment at levels of authority far above my own. But I can say quite readily that, in my own and my fellow pastors' experiences, the wealthier parishioners did not receive easier or quicker annulments than the less well off and the cost of an annulment was the same for all. It covered legitimate legal and secretarial fees. In the parishes I was associated with, the truly poor cases, as a matter of long-standing policy, never paid a penny. And they were the only ones who didn't pay a penny. We can justify that exception on basis of Our Lord's predilection for the poor.

I encourage any reader who is in what he or she thinks is 'an irretrievable marriage' to seek an annulment. How does one go about it? The process begins by contacting your local parish priest. The Lord's compassion does not exclude those with a broken marriage. On the other hand, one wishes that annulments would never be needed, that preparation for marriage would become at least as important as career preparation, and that the *ideal* of marriage would become the universal *reality* that, I believe, Jesus hoped for among his own covenanted followers.

Who destroyed our faith?

Recently I heard a person refer to Ireland as a post-Christian society. Post-Christian? It's an image that more properly describes conditions on mainland Europe where God has been dead, so to speak, for a long time. We are not there yet. Its use in relation to Irish culture is stretched. Responsible critics refer to Ireland as a post-Catholic society in the making. I assume they are referring to the breaking-up of the old monolithic Catholic culture and that they are pointing to the multi-faith, multi-cultural society we are in process of becoming.

Less responsible critics of the church are sure that we are fully a post-Catholic society already. They insist on using the phrase in a cheap psychological way to try to shunt the voice of the church off to the margins of public debate. They like to assume that the Catholic thing is gone forever; that the old Catholic hegemony is, happily, destroyed. After all, it kept us a backward people for too long. These critics fail to realise, or just will not accept the fact, that in a democracy every voice is equal and every voice has the right to contribute to the public debate and to the formation of society's values and priorities. And that includes the voice of the church.

These particular critics of the church harp on the label post-Catholic to hasten the advent of a secular society in Ireland by brain-washing people into believing it's already fully a fact and that practising Catholic people should see themselves as a kind of Irish cultural debris and get out of the way.

Of much more importance to ordinary people is the question: Is the old simple faith that we knew destroyed, the faith which we say our fathers cherished? I suppose most people think so. The faith certainly isn't what it used to be. I've even heard who destroyed it. Vatican II is a prime culprit. The Celtic Tiger is another. The

Sexual Revolution. Democracy. Education. An elderly priest said to me: 'It's the damned Redemptorists. They sowed the seeds of rejection with their warped sermons.'

I believe that the simple faith of the past is gone forever. Parts of it I miss; parts I don't. I miss the certainty. I miss the simplicity. I miss the familiar. I know these are loaded admissions to a psychologist. What have I really lost? Psychologists might say I have lost only a childish security blanket that needed to be outgrown anyway. Many other Irish seem to have lost their security blankets too. The things I say I miss may indicate that I am fundamentally an unliberated person. I'm not sure. Psychological interpretations are easy today and may be jaundiced by the liberal spirit of the age. Maybe what I miss is childhood.

I surely don't miss the puritanism of that simple faith. I don't miss the scrupulosity that always threatened my relationship with God. I don't miss the parish sermons that were inept and the mission sermons that were extreme. I don't miss the pre-occupation with dying and death and judgement; with pain, purgatory, heaven and hell; and an awful avenging God.

Above all, I don't miss the fear, the fright that the missioner tried to instil in me when I was a malleable child. I was an altar boy. I was sitting there on the cold marble step of the side altar by the sacristy in the old Athenry church. I don't think I was supposed to be there. It was Lent; it was the mission for men; and I was half-frozen. And he was up there in the pulpit, the Redemptorist, pummelling the men of the parish with a God of Judgement Day whose eye, he roared, missed nothing and whose exacting justice would have to be satisfied to the last undotted 'i' on that dread day.

He said it with such fury and such infallibility! How could he talk like that to my father and the other Guards? – great men altogether, my mother said. And how could he seem to point a finger at Dr Finnerty and Mr Corbett and Mr Sweeney and poor Michael Higgins who only rang the Protestant bell on Sunday for Canon Bomford? – a good deed to be sure, Mr King our teacher told us. He was breaking down my child's theology even though I may have never heard of that big word. He was ruining my God, the baby Jesus in the crib, that my mother said was the real God who would always love me to bits no matter what.

I remember, so clearly, that I found the preacher's words frightening at first, and then infuriating. I was only a child but I remember that I rejected his adult words in anger. In the sacristy after it was all over, I thought I might have committed a sin like Judas because the voice of God, we were told, was in the missioner and I rejected it. But that didn't last long. There was the other God of my mother, the real God, and he assured me there and then of his everlasting love, and that my father and the Guards and Dr Finnerty and Mr Sweeney and Mr Corbett and Michael Higgins were as great and as good as my mother said they were.

Did something happen then and there in terms of my future life? I don't know. Perhaps nothing happened at all. Or perhaps I took the first step on the road to a lifelong interest in theology. And perhaps there and then was formed the bias that I bring to my reading of theology no matter how speculative or mystical it may be: what is its practical meaning for my life and for parish ministry with the people? Here, perhaps, was the origin of my later style of teaching and preaching, the appeal to the heart through the head rather than an appeal to the heart through pulpit histrionics and the fantastic stories that play a dangerous game with people's emotions.

Perhaps, too, I became aware for the first time of how God is perceived and misperceived by people whether by others or by myself; how we can never really harness God and re-make him in our own image and likeness – although we're always trying to do it; how he can be heretically defined even by his orthodox promoters; how he can be enlarged or reduced by any one of us; that we need not always accept the God of some bishop or priest or missioner simply because he has an official mandate; and that one may never dare to speak with finality about God or about where people stand in their conscience before him. And because some of that sounds a bit Protestant, I've carried a healthy respect for the old Reformers with me through my priestly life. If any or all of this goes back in its origins to that awful sermon, I thank the Redemptorists. They destroyed the old, simple and unquestioning Catholic faith in me, though that was far from their intention.

So much for the old unquestioned faith. What about the old unquestioned church? Vatican II destroyed the unquestioned church. Part of the old simple faith was a view of the church that made it practically interchangeable with God. The church was God's special institution, Christ's beloved bride. It was one, holy, apostolic, singular, divine and changeless. It had the truth. It was infallible. Apart from it there was no salvation. All of this is, in fact, still true but not in the way we were taught. Priests and people understood the church and its attributes to be exclusive and absolute. In addition, the church committed no sins, made no mistakes, championed everything that was good in life, and had nothing to learn from the world. Then Vatican II spoke of the sins and mistakes of a pilgrim church, encouraged it to look to the world for forgiveness, and to the secular sciences and to the arts for help in its mission. It was a re-defined church. It was helping and hobbling at the same time through history. The perfect church was gone!

Since Vatican II we have been allowed to become familiar with the tainted history of the church. A trawl through the record of its earthly pilgrimage leaves some people aghast. Others, who are aware of human weakness, are not aghast but are nonetheless disturbed in faith over the church's displays of spiritual pride and arrogance, its role in political despotism, inquisitions, crusades, anti-Jewish pogroms, Protestant victimisations and so on. This church has often denied people their human rights and opposed the civil structures that we take for granted today and that seem so self-evident.

The moral authority of the institutional church is seriously questioned because of this history and the questioning is increased by the sins and the confusion of recent years. The admiration of old never questioned the splendour of the church and the dominance of the clergy. It also never seemed to notice the impoverished spirituality, the parrot answers, the mechanical grace and the pious platitudes. Or did it, saying nothing? All that is gone. It really was an insult to intelligent Christianity anyway, and it robbed people of the great joy of possessing a mature, reflected-upon faith.

The old faith, in that sense, is gone. In truth, it should never have seen the light of a single day. But what of the new faith? As yet, the new faith is not fully developed and it has many forms. Is it truly Christian faith? Or is a mixture of many things – what theologians call an eclectic or a selective faith?

It is not my place to pass judgement on the people who express it. People should be given an A for effort if nothing else. But I will make a few suggestions on what I think the content of this new Irish faith ought to contain because that is expected of me by those who asked this question. Three major aspects of the new Irish faith are these. Firstly, it tends to disconnect itself too much from the sacramental life of the church. Secondly, it tends to rely on forms of spirituality that are superficial or ones that avoid the discipline required by the gospels and by the saintly spiritual guides for a genuine transformation of oneself in Christ. Thirdly, its God tends to be remade a bit too much in our image and likeness.

The new faith, if it is to be Christian faith, needs to stay connected with the church, its liturgy, its sacraments and its shepherding even if it must avoid the ecclesiastical smothering of old. It is a faith that is hard-won precisely because of the church's history, its sins and unexpected incompetence and because of the collapse of trust in the church as in other public institutions. People feel that they can never again blindly trust or blindly obey any of them. This new faith is honest, personal, deliberately chosen and owned, intelligent, more and more biblically-based, reflective, and responsible. It is a mature faith and an adult faith from the standpoint of developmental psychology. Perhaps it is a purer faith such as God always meant our faith to be, devoid of the parrot and cant, the pomp and platitude. By an irony of God's grace, the faith has been renewed in part by the long-standing concerns of dissidents and Protestants who, four hundred years ago, were the Catholic Church's own protesting children and who were shunted off to the side. Too bad they were not listened to at the time.

Nevertheless, the new faith to be Christian faith needs to stay connected with the church, its liturgy, its sacraments and its shepherding. Otherwise, this new faith may become so personalised that it lapses into a purely private religion. In the same way, the new faith in order to be Christian faith expresses a Christian spirituality and not a vague New Age one or a vague Celtic one.

People are spiritual today as they always have been. The spiritual is in our blood. People's expression of the spiritual is varied at the moment and in flux. It is characterised by searching and experimentation. The New Age spiritualities are efforts at finding a spiritual expression that is personal and holistic, enriching for body, mind and spirit. New Age spiritualists are people who find traditional Christian spirituality to be too narrow, dogmatic and impersonal. Such spirituality suits neither their personal psychology nor contemporary ideals and awarenesses. As a result, New Age spirituality is not related to Christ and to the sacramental life of the church.

Celtic spirituality is another popular spirituality. In its case it is not a rejection of Christ and church life but a sincere effort to revitalise our relationships with them and to bring a sort of liturgy of nature into the scheme of things. It is a re-visiting of the old Celtic Christian vision and it may be described as a creation spirituality. Its themes happily match modern concerns – nature, the environment, ecology, the unity of all life, and praise for the gifts of creation around us. It is, therefore, a spirituality of the praise of God and of our rootedness in the earth, of our connectedness not only with other humans but with all of God's creation. All that is superb.

But if it is to stay the course as Christian spirituality for the new faith and an authentic expression of Christian faith, it must be presented in a way that is honest to its ancestry and it needs to be expanded by the full Christian theology it lacks. The whole world seems to be on a sort of Celtic binge at the minute and all kinds of commercial and religious enterprises are cashing in on the golden Celtic moment. One writer speaks of 'the proliferation of massive charlatanry in the guise of Celtic spirituality.'[3] Certainly, some of the books I read on Celtic spirituality are more imaginative and poetical than theological and authentically Christian.

Here, let me give you my opinion – it is only an opinion – on the weaknesses and strengths of Celtic spirituality as it is presently offered. Some of these weaknesses can be cleared up by down-sizing the poetry it is presently smothered in; others can be cleared-up only by adding more Christian content. For in my view Celtic spirituality, new or old, has limitations.

I find that despite the huge number of our Celtic saints we have few writings from them or from their contemporaries about them, and these writings are either questionable or theologically limited. I do not think that there is enough in them on which to develop a full Christian spirituality for the new faith. These saints are almost unknowable because of the myth and legend and fantasy that envelops them and their teachings and their actions.

More critically, these saints, assumed to be spiritual masters, lived harsh lives close to nature and yet they seem heedless of the harsher realities of nature's landscape and the hard questions that nature has for the theologian or for the believer who wants to develop a spirituality that cannot easily lapse into religious escapism. Nature's often brutal and systemic realities are present to young and old today in their classroom studies and in living colour on TV. But they are not present to the old Celtic landscape, at least not to the one that has come down to us covered in myth, convenient miracle and fantasy. It may well be that these saints have been overly romanticised and that nature, as they *really* experienced it, has been sanitised by those who give us the accounts of their lives and of their spiritual combat.

In the same way, the Celtic spirituality of the present day lives mostly on the surface of things. Now it is easy to transfigure pleasing surfaces – 'the cathedral of the outdoors' – into poetry or into the praise of God. But there is no sifting eye of a Darwin or of a Liam O'Flaherty or of a St Paul on this landscape, no coming to grips with nature's rawness and contradictions and with the evidence of the scars of original sin on it. Celtic spirituality, old and new, lacks this realism of nature. Hence, it is a nature that is not particularly in need of Christian redemption.

Is this the reason why Celtic spirituality, new or ancient, has no reaching down into the biblical depth of things, no rugged cross set as a redemptive necessity into the earth as a sign that, with men and women, 'all creation groans and is in agony' (Rom 8:22)? It has its high crosses to be sure but they are things of crafted beauty on the pleasant landscape. Celtic prayer invokes the cross to be sure but is it only as a sign of personal salvation, protection and blessing? The Celtic cross is not related in a redemptive way to nature because nature is not seen to be in need of it. If, then, Celtic spirituality does not address *all* creation as fallen, it has no Christian inscape by which to grace nature's troublesome theology. Authentic transfiguration begins at this deeper level. And it should. After all, we are tied to a Christ who died in crisis and in blood on wood and iron.

In contrast, Vatican II's *Lumen Gentium* (#48) ties all creation to humanity in the Fall and hence under the redemption of the cross. And so, wounded creation groans but may look forward to a time when 'together with the human race, the universe itself, which is so closely related to man and which attains its destiny through him, will be perfectly re-established in Christ (cf. Ephes 1:10; Col 1:20; 2 Pt 3:10-13).'

Celtic spirituality, as presently offered, shies away from such hard questions and it lacks full Christian definition. It is too lyrical as theology and too much in the 'feel good' category as spirituality. It needs to expand itself theologically along the lines we have been indicating. It also needs to avoid the obscurity that would allow its proponents, if they wished, to direct their praise and thanks to a vague dynamic in nature which might be identified as God but hardly as the personal God of Christ. Opaque is the colour of much contemporary spirituality.

The value of Celtic spirituality, in Christian terms, is not so much in its treatment of nature but in its treatment of God and the human. Its strengths are, first of all, its praise theology. Praise of God is foundational to our faith and acknowledgement of the creator God is the primary gesture of the Judeo-Christian religion. A second strength is its view of time as continuous and our several worlds as interrelated. Old Celtic spirituality's mind-set saw no barriers between worlds and moved with ease between heaven and earth, the eternity of God and time-bound man, spirits and angels and fairies and the dead, this life and the next, the realms of human and animal, as though one passed merely from room to room in the same house. Today, we need all sorts of barriers to be minimalised, if not removed fully, in the same way. I'm thinking of the North for one thing. We need to reconnect God and human beings, the secular and the sacred, this life and the next as a unity; and we need a deep sense of human solidarity and greater respect for life, air, landscape, soil and water. Our plastic-draped hedges are a small illustration of the need. There is no better place to find the model for all of this than in ancient Celtic spirituality.

Celtic spirituality promotes just and caring human relationships. It promotes nurturing, fostering and hospitality in general. These speak to the political and social divisions of our time, to the hurts endured from abuse, victimisation and broken relationships. It should not be too difficult to extend this attitude and this practice to include asylum seekers, refugees and migrants of all kinds.

The opposite of this cherished old Celtic practice is a relapse into selfishness and greed. Is this not the temptation of the Celtic Tiger and of the golden moment?

The new faith rejects the avenging God of the past. It emphasises the God of love. This is as it should be. For 'God is love' (1 Jn 4:16) and we Irish are as spiritually exhausted from our years of dealing with an avenging Lord as we are from dealing with generations of loveless landlords. But the new faith must be careful how it understands this love lest it find itself divorced from the authentic Christian tradition.

It is standard fare in the church now to stress the unconditional nature of God's love. Taking this as their cue, some in their new faith are certain that God's love is so unconditional that we must no longer speak of any limitations at all on it. The practical implication of this, they say, is that we must abandon the old theological constructs of punishment, pain, purgatory and hell. Talk of pain and punishment, of purgatory and hell, they feel, only re-introduces the old avenging God. He does not fit into our latest pleasant landscape of large comfortable homes that reflect large comfortable minds and hearts tempted to pursue a cross-less, comfortable theology. Pain is the great modern no-no. God's unconditional love should be just that: a love without limits and without avenging consequences.

The church also believes in God's unconditional love for us but understands it differently. God's love is unconditional from his point of view. But we force him to be a God of justice and of punishment because of our sinful actions. We are morally responsible for our behaviour. Immoral actions invoke God's rule of justice. Actions have consequences. That's a fact of life. The new faith shouldn't try to avoid it.

St Paul writes: 'For we will all stand before the judgment seat of God ... each of us will be accountable to God.' (Rom 14: 10, 12) The church, therefore, will not let go of the God of justice even as it promotes the God of unconditional love. For the church, God's love is unconditional in itself but it is conditioned by the freedom of response he has respected us with. Our response is sometimes sinful. And it is accountable. One must take the totality of the revelation given us in the scriptures in order to appreciate how God's unconditional love is to be understood. It is unconditional with God: it is conditioned by us.

The church's interpretation, following the scriptures, is not a kind one for those of the new faith who want no limits on God's love. But, then, many of the scriptures about God are not too kind from our lax or increasingly sophisticated point of view. They will become even less kind and less acceptable to us as our society prospers even more.

People in the new faith say that the God of unconditional love cannot by definition be a punisher no matter what the church or the scriptures say. Besides, what mortal sin committed in a moment, no matter how dreadful, calls for an eternity of punishment from any God, whether it is the God of unconditional love or one of justice?

The church will not give way on this point. The church is tied to its scriptures and it will be faithful to them as it understands them. Therefore, the church's answers to our questions must at times be hard, even unacceptable by human reasoning, acceptable only through faith.

Therefore, the new faith, to be Christian faith, is called to the disclosure and to the discipline of God's revealed word in scripture. There we find the answers and the limitations of the answers which God has revealed for us. He judges them sufficient to our pilgrim needs. We may not select only our favourites from among them. God is love – yes. His love is covenanted and it is unconditional – yes. Our actions have consequences in time and in eternity – yes. There is a hell – yes. And there is a process of purification after death, as in the Second Book of Maccabees of the Catholic version of the bible, which is called purgatory – yes. So, the new faith, to be Christian faith, cannot construct a God divorced from scripture and church, a soft God, a soft love, a morality without consequences, and an afterlife without the constructs of heaven, hell and purgatory. Nor may the new faith allow real faith to simply avoid the whole issue by ignoring unsuitable scriptures. That is a tendency of the new faith in Ireland.

Is that all there is to it, then? Must the new faith live with these old theologies of punishment, hell and purgatory that sound so vicious and primitive in their fire and brimstone? For our purposes, as scripture sees it, yes. But perhaps a better understanding of the nature of pain and punishment in the afterlife might help. It is true that scripture describes these in the physical terms of place, fire and torture. Scripture often describes spiritual realities by physical imagery. Surely this language can be understood as culturally conditioned, as our ancestors' way of describing spiritual realities in physical terms and by analogy with their space-time experiences? If so, it is possible to read the New Testament and to conclude that the physicality of purgatory and hell as places of fire is really incidental.

One can read the scriptures and sense that the pain and punishment are more properly understood in psychological and spiritual frames. Purgatory and hell may be understood as profound realisations of profound losses. In this understanding the essence of purgatory's fire is the soul's realisation of the horror of its sins, and the essence of the fire of hell is the soul's realisation of its now utterly hopeless condition. We read in the *Catechism of the Catholic Church:* 'The chief punishment of hell is eternal separation from God, in whom alone man can possess the life and happiness for which he was created and for which he longs.'[4] And the *Catechism* reminds us that the church's teachings on purgatory and hell are not there for the purpose of arguing over the love and the justice of God but are there as 'a call to the responsibility' of making use of our freedom 'in view of [our] eternal destiny,' and as 'an urgent call to conversion'.

None of this may satisfy people of the new faith because it still leaves purgatory and hell – and a vindicating God – intact. They want a future without them. Is any other future possible? Is there a future beyond the bible's revelation of the future that we are locked into at the moment? Is there a last level of things, a final resolution of all, which is not part of the revelation given us in scripture?

There does not appear to be if we stay within the limits of the scriptures. But, then, who knows the depth of the mind and the heart of God? No one, I believe. In dealing specifically with God's mercy, the bible exclaims: 'O the depth of the riches and wisdom and knowledge of God! How unsearchable are his judgments and how inscrutable his ways!' (Rom 11:33) If the church has quietly put aside limbo as a finality for the unbaptised infants, and if it has added the entirely new dimension of the hope of blessedness for them beyond death, cannot the God of unconditional love have a further stage to his saving plan for adults? He certainly can, and he certainly may. It is not for me to say. In the meanwhile, the new faith, like the old faith, follows the narrower road and lives within the parameters of that future that the scriptures have unfolded for us.

All the bloody religious wars

One thing that the troubles in the North did was to raise the question: Does religion cause wars? There have been many religious wars and they are an embarrassment to a believer and a stumbling block to faith for contemporary men and women. I'm not going to give a simple answer and neatly divorce religion from war and say that there is no connection between the two. Religion tends to slip out of the messy questions by absolving itself and fingering someone else. The stock answer of the church is no. War, says the church, is the result of many other things such as sin and racism, politics, pride and extreme nationalism, ambition, territorial and economic greed, and vengeance. So far so good.

But what about the 'holy' wars like the crusades? You are told that the wars of the crusaders were religious liberation movements which sought to win back the holy places associated with Christ or, at least, to guarantee free passage to Christian pilgrims. If you mention the plethora of Islamic *jihads* you are told these also are liberation movements or they are the defensive battles of a great religion for its cultural values. If you mention sectarian war in regard to the North you are told that the war there is political and economic and only incidentally religious.

The plain fact is that Catholics and Protestants have fought wars in Europe in which religion was the main issue and politics and economics only secondary ingredients. Muslims and Hindus have fought brutal wars. Islam and Christianity have done the same and with the same priority of interests. If you look in some detail at a number of wars of independence you will notice that in some of them religion is paramount. Religion seems to give war an added zeal, ferocity and brutality. We saw this recently in East Timor with Muslims and Christians. We saw it in religiously-fractured Yugoslavia.

The villains of these wars are, let's face it, religious people. They appear to be committed to God. In fact, some of them are happy to die for God. And they are happy to slaughter all around them in God's name. Something is very wrong here and it does not help the world to have its religious leaders hide their heads in the sand and pretend that something other than religion is the cause of it.

It is not enough for religious leaders to quote their various sacred scriptures (they all have holy scriptures) or their latest official documents on avoiding war and cherishing peace. The hard fact is that these teachings have yet to influence their followers in a way that converts their hearts. Every religion is full of beautiful stuff that is not translated into reality on the ground. That's the heart of the matter. Will it ever be? *Can* it ever be?

Is there something in religion – a hidden dynamic – that necessarily pushes people towards violence and war? There doesn't seem to be. The historians Will and Ariel Durant, who have the additional talent of the philosopher, say: 'The causes of war are the same as the causes of competition among individuals: acquisitiveness, pugnacity, and pride; the desire for food, land, materials, fuels, mastery.'[5]

All of us have the instinct of belligerence but it is not a hidden thing and it is not, of its nature, a religious thing. Social historians, psychologists and theologians are familiar with this instinct just as we are ourselves from our own life experience. Warmongering may be something in the genes from time immemorial. It may be an old aggressive instinct now difficult to moderate. It may be the consequence of original sin, as in the church's explanation.

When we look at the greatest war in history, World War II, historians do not make religion its cause. Militarism, expansionism, racism, revenge and xenophobic nationalism were some obvious causes. Religion, even though it was a part of German culture as it is of all cultures, does not seem to have had any influence. The majority of Germans were baptised Christians for sure, but that did not cause their going to war or their national pride or their felt need to undo what they believed to be the insult and the injury of the Treaty of Versailles. Hitler's solution of his so-called Jewish problem was not a religion-related issue for him or for his clique. The anti-Jewish bias of German and Christian history may well have been a factor in allowing the German people to acquiesce in the slaughter of the Jewish people, but it was not a formative cause of the Second World War.

Is the idea of a religious war, a war of religious aggression, with its particularly fanatical ardour, a failure to understand the real God and real theology? I think the answer has to be yes. But it is not an easy answer. Here's why. All of us believers are tied to the bible as God's revealed word. Now the God of the Old Testament is not always a gentle God. In fact, he is the God of armies and of war. He is the God most often quoted by the General Pattons of western history. Not for them the gentle Jesus of the New Testament!

The God of Israel appears to do all the wrong things. He ethnically cleanses the Canaanites from their land so that it can become the promised land of Israel. He holds the waters of the sea apart so that the Israelites escape dryshod through it. Then he lets the waters fall back into place so that the pursuing Egyptian army can be eliminated as the walls of water fall in on them. He is the God who fights Israel's wars and approves the plundering and the purging of Israel's enemies. The bible expects him, presumably, to accept the prayer of the man of faith who asks that the heads of his enemies' children be smashed on the stones. All through the Old Testament God is fighting wars, presumably holy wars, but wars nevertheless. The Old Testament God is a Warrior God. He is the Lord of armies and the God of battles.

It was easy, then, with this template from the bible, for the church to send the crusaders to war. It was easy for the aggrandising 'Christian' nations of Europe to collect their empires through war and slaughter and subjugation. They were extending civilisation and enlightenment. They were even extending Christianity. So their public relations said. All they had to do was to underpin their imperialism and their conquest with the theology of the God of Battles and to have a view of their enemies, be they Hindu or Papist, as ungodly people. Kipling echoed this biblical theology of the Warrior God in his *Recessional* when he wrote in 1897:

God of our fathers, known of old,
Lord of our far-flung battle-line,
Beneath whose awful hand we hold
Dominion over palm and pine.

And because he sensed in 1897 that the empire was being taken for granted, or that God and social responsibility were being ignored in the flush of empire, or that he himself had become uncomfortable with the theology that anchored empire, he added sombrely:

Lord God of Hosts, be with us yet,
Less we forget – less we forget!

We have to move beyond the Old Testament and into the New Testament (or we have to regard God's action in regard to Israel as something unique) in order to answer the question: Is the idea of a religious war a failure to understand the real God and real theology? There is little question that God's focus changes as we move from testament to testament. Even in the later books of the Old Testament he is already becoming less bellicose. He begins to assume the characteristics that we today associate with him. He becomes paternal and even maternal. Finally, in Christ, he becomes the God of each one and everyone, the forgiving, caring, comforting Father of all his human children.

Jesus brings this gradually unfolding process to a climax when he reveals God as the God of love. The New Testament God is not a Lord of Battles but the Lord of love. His kingdom is not political. It is a kingdom of the heart. It is a kingdom of love and peace and justice. It is impossible to associate this God of Jesus with any war of aggression or any war based on religion. It is, of course, an entirely different matter to call on the Lord's protection in a defensive war, assuming you have not provoked it in the first place.

Religious wars have been a constant in history and they continue today. They are an insult to the God of love, they give religion a bad name, they define religion as irrational and volatile, and they keep intelligent and well-meaning people distant from God. The world is still awash with religious wars because of a failure in the religious leadership and because of a failure in religious education at its most basic level.

I am well aware of some of the difficulties in surmounting this failure. Religion is tied to emotion. Religion is tied to culture. Religion gets mixed up with patriotism. Religion gets mixed up with politics. The religious instinct is appealed to and stirred up by tyrants and by thugs. Religion is filtered by mind-set. Mature religion, just like mature moral judgement, presupposes reflection. A lot of religion is not reflected upon by an awful lot of religionists. One's own personal psychology is critical in how religion is used or abused. So is the legacy of one's religious history with its weight of traditional enemies and its lists of the sacrificed dead. There is the burden of past religious injustices done to your ancestors and old scores yet to be settled. Religion exists in many people only in its most primitive, biased and explosive forms. These are reasons why issues of war are sometimes complex and why religion often gets mixed up in them. They are the reasons why we still have crusades, *jihads* and religious wars.

Yes, religious authorities must face up to the challenge of educating their adherents. They must confront their adherents with religion as love and with the holy war as a theological – certainly a Christian – anachronism. They must convert the 'holy' warlords who are the triggers of these modern religious wars. These 'holy' warlords are the ones who so easily stir up their millions of foot soldiers, the poor, uneducated believers who are the most intellectually famished and exploited people on earth.

These warlords know perfectly well what they are doing to their people and to God. We see nearly all of them sooner or later on TV explaining themselves and their high holy purposes. They praise their God and they quote their sacred books. They speak two or three languages. They are quite educated and quite articulate. They know full well the wrong they are doing in the name of God and of religion.

The Tiger gave us what God didn't

Nearly all of us have been blessed by the Celtic Tiger. To pretend otherwise is to forget our dismal economic history. So many of our tears have been the result of emigration, an exodus because of famine sure enough, but much of it a flight from grinding poverty.

When I told my mother in the mid-1950s that I was going to go to Maynooth she was elated. 'Your father and I will play the fiddle in the streets if that's what it takes to pay your way.' I knew they couldn't pay my way and I knew she couldn't play the fiddle. A month later, when I said I was going to the American mission instead, she said: 'You'll always have a penny in your pocket.' I knew what she was thinking. Ireland was full of young priests, a stagnant economy and a dwindling population. She was thinking of her child's welfare. He would be better off abroad. Her tears would come later.

How many rosaries were said, how many penny candles were lit over the Irish generations praying for release from poverty? How many novenas were done scrupulously for a job for which there were too many applicants, and how many Masses were offered for a state in life, as it was put, that would give the son or the daughter the security of steady work and maybe a tiny pension in the end?

There are two ways of looking at all this prayer and what happened to it. First, you could say it wasn't answered. It was not answered in its time and place for so many who had to take the boat. You could say, as many do now, that God didn't answer our prayers but the Celtic Tiger did. So, why should we make a big deal out of God and religion anymore? Sláinte to the Tiger! He (or she) did it all for us.

I think that's a good part of young Ireland's quandary with the faith today. Prayer gave it nothing; the multi-nationals did. Ours was a religion of petition because of our basic human needs. What was more basic than the need of a job? The religion of petition failed us in that. So we may not have lost our belief in God's existence but we've lost faith in God as a friend, as the proverbial *anam chara,* as someone really concerned for our welfare. Most of traditional Irish theology is a theology of petition, geared to need, to economics, limited to getting things. In that narrow theology, God proved to be an absent God for us.

In saying that, we are not trying to be philosophical or smart. We are not making it an excuse for our declining church attendances. It's just that God defined himself for us in our need as an absent God through our experiences with him. Should we not have known that we were reducing God in this way to the measure of economics and thus setting a trap for our faith? After all, the God of economics is not the most prominent God in the bible. But, I'm afraid, he is the reduced God that was taught to us in the theology of endless Masses, candles and novenas for a job. And he still is so presented to a great degree.

On the other hand, it could be said that God finally answered all the prayer, not individually and piecemeal, but in a collective way for the nation and the people as a whole. We're not trying to be smart here either and let God off the hook. The biblical God of deliverance works with the nation more than with the individual. That's how he is depicted in the record we have of his actions in history. The emphasis in the bible is on the people rather than on the individual. It is on the nation of Israel rather than on individual Israelites. Ireland's need was not for an individual job here and there in an anaemic economy that generated exile for the masses. Ireland's need was always for an economy of scale and depth for the whole nation. We have it now.

Should we not assume then, based on the bible's paradigm, that God answered our prayers on the grand scale, and should we not be grateful to him for it? And do we appreciate from our economic studies that a nation's economy, no matter how internally strong or how multi-nationally anchored, remains subject to political and natural forces that can depress it at any time? In the global economy a small nation is always at risk. Are we praying to God that the Celtic Tiger continues? Or are we just downing our gins-and-tonic and assuming that it will?

If God has answered all the prayer, not piecemeal but collectively for the whole nation, then he was not an absent God in the prayer partnership at all but a very concerned one. And he delivered. The proof is all around us. In this scenario, what must he make of the new Irish silence in his regard and our loss of faith in him as a friend?

I would like it if the church were more positive about the Celtic Tiger and helped people, especially the young, to see the hand of God in it. The bishops have written along these lines to be sure, but who reads them? I asked thirty-six adults in one class if they had read anything more than a headline by the bishops on the Celtic Tiger. No one had. A Christian suspicion lingers about the Tiger. I sometimes see an article or a quote from some sermon that accuses the Tiger of being a pagan thing that is leading us away from God. We are told that the Tiger has us by the tail, that he's the latest blight on us from the devil. In fact, that he may be the devil in disguise.

I remember – with sadness more than anger – too many Irish sermons on moral blight to take this one seriously. The devil is trivialised when he is made the inventor of the Celtic Tiger. He was trivialised in the same way in the past when sermons berated him as the inventor of such things as the camera, Hollywood, nylon stockings, Brylcream and bicycle clips for the lads, the song 'Goodnight, Irene,' the tango, ballroom dancing and even Fr Horan's dancehall (the devil appeared there in person!) down in Mayo. Anything new or challenging to some religionists is said to come from Satan. I believe most of it comes from God. Why are such sermons and suggestions still made? Maybe it's because the condemnatory form of preaching is the laziest and least spiritually constructive form there is.

I take the Tiger as a blessing from God, not a curse from the devil. What does one do with a blessing? Accept it. Be grateful for it. Give thanks. Use it to enhance oneself and others. We stayed close to God in our poverty; now let the church show us how to stay close to him in the new economy of our wealth.

I remember a parishioner who once said to me, 'It's a shame that so many bad people have so much of the world's wealth. It's too bad that enough good people don't have it. They could do so much good with it.' He's right. It could be a wonderful world if the right people had the money. But, you might object, 'Is money not the root of all evil? Doesn't scripture say that somewhere?' It doesn't. It says something quite different. It says 'the *love* of money is a root of all kinds of evil.' (1 Tim 6:10) Money in itself is morally neutral. It can be used for good or evil. It's making a greedy god of it and how you get it and what you do with it that matter.

I've never wanted to have a lot of money myself. There's probably a whole psychology to this that I am not aware of. One facet of it is clear enough to me. It's my mother saying as I went to America, 'Remember, your health is your wealth.' Another facet is an aunt who said of her neighbours, 'You watch; the money will turn their heads.' A third and indelible one is the etching that was in our history book in the national school in Athenry. It is the etching of a top-hatted landlord or a bailiff on his horse. There are police at hand and there are men with a battering ram. They are there to tumble the hovel of a poor tenant and his family. The poor family had survived the Famine only to be levelled by this sin of wealth.

Ever since then I am conscious that wealth is not a matter of evil but a terrible personal and social responsibility. I can do with just enough to get by with. I pray that those who have a lot will have the wisdom to know how to spend it. Being wealthy is a huge moral responsibility and a headache. I know that young people may not see it that way, but it is.

Our new wealth has its opportunities and its responsibilities for the nation and for us. Here are a few examples. With this wealth our families can have better housing, care, health, education and opportunities in life. This is the stuff of generations of Irish prayers. Ideally, this wealth will make us Irish more sociable and more Christian because poverty sits no more on our doorstep. Ideally, we will be as generous to refugees and asylum seekers and migrant workers as we were when, though poor, we reached out to strangers in distant lands through the old foreign mission appeals. Ideally, we will be as generous to them as other nations have been to us in taking in generations of our uncles and aunts, and sons and daughters. Ideally, we will use our new wealth to enhance our culture in all its best artistic and religious forms.

Ideally, we will be grateful to God every day for his gift. And we will not become the twenty-first century's version of those in the scripture who knew God's presence in their poverty and lost him in their wealth.

Why doesn't God speak up more?

Those who ask this question say that if God expects us to have a relationship with him he ought to make himself better known. Why doesn't he?

Bertrand Russell, the philosopher, didn't believe in God. When challenged as to what he would say if he found God waiting for him in the next life, he said he would tell him that he didn't give us enough signs of himself. Or words to that effect. In other words, Russell would not accept personal blame for being an atheist. God is the cause of our atheism and agnosticism because he doesn't communicate with us enough or clearly. St Teresa, the mystic, was a believer. She persevered in her struggle for intimacy with the Lord even though she had to suffer a lot from his silences. 'No wonder you have so few friends,' she said.

People today hate obscurity and prize clarity. This is especially true, I think, when others start making claims on us: claiming our acceptance of them, claiming a relationship with us, claiming our trust, claiming our loyalty, claiming our love. God claims all of these and our very lives and souls too. So why doesn't he make himself better known to us?

If a company headhunts me I'm not going to just take it as a compliment and sign-on immediately. I want to know everything about that company from A to Z. If God wants me to believe in him – and to have a personal relationship and spiritual intimacy with him – is he not expecting an awful lot, based on too little showing of himself? People today do not experience him as exactly a quantifiable, up-front, hands-on sort of person. They feel that God is too vague, too distant and too silent. He doesn't give us enough signs of his presence, as Lord Russell said.

The same argument about vagueness and distance and silence

can be used against the church. It makes remarkable claims on us. It claims to have God's unique word for us. It claims to be able to show us God's way. It expects our submission to its authority and to its enlightenment. Yet, it doesn't always speak convincingly or clearly. It has a somewhat obscure theology on many issues and the more it is challenged by the young, the more it seems to retreat into obscurity and the more its language becomes oblique. It has limitations in so far as rational analysis, human experience and sometimes common sense are concerned. At some point conversation becomes a dead-end, at least to a generation educated to hate obscurity and to prize clarity, a questioning and a communications age.

On the other hand, it can be argued that God does, in fact, do a lot of showing of himself and a lot of speaking up. Maybe we have lost the ability to listen despite all the talk about clarity and communications. Let's be fair to God. He is always active in the partnership with us.

God comes into our lives in many ways. First, there is the fundamental level on which God meets us. It is the level at which he first discloses himself to us. It is the level of his first communication with us. This first communication may be a kind of formless assurance of his presence and love in our depths but it is very real and experiential. It is a level that is deeper than the silences that disturb us. It is a level deeper than all the questions we have. It is a communication of God and a self-disclosure of God to us prior to all scripture and theology and even formal language. Scripture and theology flesh it out of course: they are subsequent and fuller disclosures by God about himself and his love for us.

In our very nature God fashioned us in such a way that he is already in our being showing himself and speaking with us, antecedently of all revelation and theology. This fundamental fact is alluded to in the Psalms: 'Be still, and know that I am God.' (Ps 46:11) Be still and you will know that I am present to you, speaking within you, and there to be for you. Every one of us can experience God in this way and every one of us has from time to time. For many among us it is a daily experience and a reassuring one.

Theologians (such as Martin Buber and Karl Rahner) explain the phenomenon this way. We look at our human nature and at the nature of communication. We find that communication is very natural to us. It is so natural that it is essential to our human definition. It is of our very being. We are defined by our need to communicate with others. We have an innate 'openness' to others because we are social beings at our core and not individuals standing all alone. We have a fundamental need to address and to speak to others and to be addressed and to be spoken to by them. This speaking can be words or signs or gestures or presences or even silences. All of them are idioms of communication. Here, too, at the core of our being is our natural openness to God. He is an Other to be addressed and spoken with. In fact, the openness to others that is in us is, first of all, an openness for communication with God. He put it there.

We've all had experiences at times of sensing God in our depths, of talking with him and he with us, however vaguely, and of being stirred to wonder about ourselves and life, and stirred to ask fundamental questions from that depth in us. These fundamental questions are not about science and art and football and the weather or the beat on the street. They are theological questions even if we cannot spell that word. They are about God and us and our relationship. And they are the stirrings of God at our core.

Religion is the relationship arising out of our openness to God and his openness to us. It is God and ourselves mutually responding to this 'openness to others' that he put in our being as a parallel image of what is in himself. This is the reason why the religious instinct is not superficial but is in us at our core. And it is in us as a principle of communication and relationship between ourselves and God.

Religion in this proper sense is not, therefore, something that we as individuals or the human race collectively have picked up by accident or by evolution. Such common explanations come too superficially and too late in the process. It was not born in us during some later history or in response to some cultural need or psychological fear. The religious principle is at our core prior to its many and varied cultural expressions in history.

Our openness or natural bent for communication allows us to be spoken to by God and to speak to him. The bible has many references to the enemies and the competitors of this inner voice. They include the pace of life, the rat race as we moderns call it, even the ordinary cares of life, the babble of a hundred voices in our ear every day and the anxieties on our minds as we go to sleep. Scripture speaks of our need to draw ourselves apart so that we can hear God's voice speaking within us in the space and silence we create for the conversation with him. 'I will … bring her [the soul] into the wilderness and speak tenderly to her.' (Hos 2:14)

The ancient Hebrews, and Jesus as a part of that tradition, were fully aware of this 'modern' theology of Buber and Rahner when they referred over and over again to God speaking to the human heart, God speaking in the silence of the heart, and God already present in the inner, secret recesses of our hearts. For all our talk about prizing communication and clarity, maybe it is we and not God who are losing our inner ear so that we cannot hear him speak to our heart and to our loneliness and to our need in a communications age that is deafening us with its storm of so many other and so many loud voices.

What I have been describing is not a spiritual condition that is experienced only by the saints. It is an openness to God at the core of every person; so much so that even those who live frenetically will still find the Lord knocking at the door of their hearts in their losses and in their loneliness and in their need. But do they listen and let him comfort them?

This openness to God, that God put in our nature as part of our openness to others, is something we seem to neglect more and more in our communications age. I think it is something which the Lord will bring forward on judgement day in contestation of any of us – and not just Bertrand Russell – who speak too readily of his absence and not of his presence. If God is radically open to me and I to him in our very natures, then he is speaking to my heart all the time. But am I listening? Do I make space in my life to listen? Communications is a two-way street.

God discloses himself to us in other ways. The prints of his presence are all over our world. So much so that St Paul felt that people should be able to come to know God through the things he has made, whether those things are the beauties of the natural world or the amazing dynamics by which constellations live. (See Rom 1:20) Now, of course, you can see all of this wonder as so many atoms and so much dust, or you can be overcome by its beauty, as the American astronaut was when he looked down on the earth and saw it framed by the darkness that marked the endlessness of space, and started quoting the book of Genesis.

In the same way you can take the seasons and the weather and birth and life and explain them by their inner dynamics and purposes, but you have not touched the miracle and the mystery and the gift and the goodness that they are. You can even face the evil and the violence that is in us and look to science – genetic engineering and cloning perhaps – as their hopeful solution, but you haven't gone to the depth of the blight. Sin is the real issue. There is nothing projected by 'spare-parts' genetics and human replication that will construct a better *moral* human being or a more sensitive human heart. We need to be restructured by God's word and grace and that has nothing to do with genes. But I don't wish to give the impression that science and technology are anything other than the helping hand of God among us. In their proper roles they certainly are. So are all the healing arts and sciences. They are all marks of the Lord's presence with us.

We read in the letter to the Hebrews:

> Long ago, God spoke to our ancestors in many and various ways by the prophets, but in these last days he has spoken to us by a Son, whom he appointed heir of all things, through whom he also created the worlds. He is the reflection of God's glory and the exact imprint of God's very being, and he sustains all things by his powerful word. (Heb 1:1-3)

Who is Jesus and why is he so important? We'll speak of him here only in terms of the argument that God does not show us enough signs of his presence.

Look at the last line quoted above. Jesus is 'the exact imprint of God's very being.' Jesus is the exact image of God. If you want to know God, study Jesus. If you wonder what God is really like, look at Jesus. If you think God is distant, understand that Jesus is 'the Word [that] became flesh and lived among us.' (Jn 1:14) If you ask whether God speaks to you with endless concern, read the gospels. They are his love letters to you. If you doubt God would die for love of you, know that God found a way to do it: look at Jesus on Calvary. God, in Jesus, has done more for me than all my wonderful family and friends rolled into one. And for two reasons: he was capable of doing more and he gave his all for me to the last drop of his blood.

The whole life of Jesus, with you and me as the focal point of his life and selfless love, is one huge display of God's print and presence expressed as a communication of love, care, concern, support and encouragement. It hasn't ended. He has left us his Spirit to whisper all these good things, and many more, to our hearts. But we must make space and listen. Those who make space and those who listen will know the Spirit speaking to their hearts every single day.

This particular love story does have the ending which, in our heart of hearts, we want all love stories to have, but which we say only happens in the dream factory that is Hollywood. Towards the end of his life on earth Jesus said, 'And if I go and prepare a place for you, I will come again and will take you to myself, so that where I am, there you may be also.' (Jn 14:3)

'Tis God's will, isn't it?

This chapter covers two questions. Why does the church teach people to accept their lot as God's will rather than fight for justice and a better life? And why are we told that everything from the Famine to your child's premature death is God's will?

It would be neat if one could say simply that none of these is God's will and that's that! But such an easy answer only raises other questions. For example, if God is not involved in some way in our tragedies as well as in our triumphs, how can we say that he is the Lord and master of all or that 'in him we live and move and have our being' (Acts 17:28)? If God is not involved in some manner in our pain as well as in our joy, are we not denying the scripture in which David says to God, 'Everything is from you.' (1 Chr 29:14)?

The question of God's will in relation to both human tragedy and natural disasters is a huge one. Here, we will stick to the specific questions asked. Perhaps my responses may also have a bearing on the larger question.

Contrary to what you may have been told, the church actually teaches that people should not accept their lot but that they should struggle for justice and a better life. This teaching is part of the church's social doctrine and is expressed in the church's call for 'human development' and 'the development of peoples'. The great proponents of human development and the development of peoples are Paul VI and John Paul II. The terms are also used in the official *Catechism of the Catholic Church.*

The church in the past may have over-emphasised the next world to the neglect of this one and thus encouraged people to put up with their lot. Today, however, this is not the case. In the Our Father we pray 'thy kingdom come'. What does this phrase mean? What is the kingdom? In the past we tended to think of it as something to do with the afterlife, with the kingdom of heaven. The kingdom is the dominion of God over our hearts, and it is his rule of love and peace and justice on this earth now and in every society. The meaning of 'thy kingdom come' is actually explained by the follow-on phrase, 'thy will be done on earth as it already is done in heaven.' We pray for the coming into our lives of God's kind dominion over us and his justice and peace and love over our world and in every strand of its political and social life. And do our lives and our poor world ever need justice and peace and love!

Just as our understanding of the kingdom has changed or enlarged, so has our understanding of the work of the gospel and of the words of Jesus, 'Go, make disciples of all the nations.' (Mt 28:19) Missionary work – bringing Christ to people and people to Christ – has two levels. In the old days, missionaries went out to evangelise. This meant that they went out to convert people to Christ and to Christianity. Today, they still go out to evangelise in that sense but they also go out to establish the kingdom of God on earth. Evangelisation is more than counting Christian heads. It's lifting people up. It's showing Christ's practical concern for them in their immediate needs and in their long-term human and social development. It's helping them in the areas of freedom and justice and education and work and jobs. This so-called social gospel is not an appendage to the gospel of Jesus but an integral part of it.

Because of the corrupt political and social conditions in many places – and because of the larger understanding of what evangelisation entails – missionaries find themselves more and more in confrontational settings not of their choosing. In their solidarity with their people they find themselves opposing poverty and injustice and confronting sinful social structures and mechanisms of oppression. These sinful structures in a given country or culture may be the entrenched and elite ruling class, the police, the military, the courts and even the government. The mechanisms of oppression are: keeping people poor, dependant on others, and locked into the political and economic interests and wars of others. Tens of millions of people around the world are terribly exploited and, as children of God, utterly marginalised in their own lands. I believe it was Pope Paul VI who first spoke of this 'vicious cycle of poverty'.

Now, in these terrible straits, a missionary might tend to neglect the conversion side of his work, or he might step over the line of non-violent development and get caught up in an armed struggle. Some have and some do. So did some priests in Central America in our time and so did Fr John Murphy with the pikemen in 1798. But such incidents are the exception. My point is that the church does not teach people to accept poverty and injustice as God's will. On the contrary, the church teaches them to work for their liberation in Christ on both the spiritual and social levels.

The response to the first question is clear enough then. The church teaches that people should *not* accept an unjust or an impoverished social condition as God's will but that they should struggle for justice and a better life.

The second question is not easy to answer. It is not easy to answer for the reasons I gave in the second paragraph of this chapter. Let's try to explore it anyway. Why are the Irish taught that everything from the Famine to your child's premature death is the will of God?

I do not have the kind of detailed knowledge of the Famine that one would need in order to accept or reject the claim that the church taught people to see the Famine as the will of God and a curse from God. There are, indeed, contemporary comments on record from individual priests and people expressing such views. However, individual comments do not amount to church teaching. Are such comments not more accurately a reflection of the psychology that invests poor, starved people who are at wits' end in the face of catastrophe? I think so.

For myself, I do not believe that God sent the Famine on our ancestors. You might feel that I am a little hesitant about that statement and wonder how I could say anything other. I am hesitant only because scripture makes me so. There is the line I already quoted from David: 'Everything is from you [God].' (1 Chr 29:14) Similarly, when Job was faced with an appalling set of tragedies he said, 'The Lord gave and the Lord has taken away.' (Job 1:21) He does not rule out the hand of God in his misery even as he searches for its cause in his own sins. In Famine times, priests and people searched themselves for the cause of their plight and some of them concluded that it was a punishment from God for their sins.

I've lived through several earthquakes in Southern California in my time. Some people saw them as God's will. They were his punishment on the supposed Godlessness of the place and its people. Others dismissed God entirely from any role in the earthquakes and the loss of life, explaining them only with reference to nature and its shifting tectonic plates. Geologically speaking, earthquakes can be explained easily and naturally. But scripture will not allow us to remove God altogether from his world, no matter how troublesome this is for God and for our faith in him. The bible has scenes of famine and natural destruction. They are brought about by human evil and sin. They are described as punishments of God.

God, as master and mover of all, cannot be removed from the dark side of life and it is an all-sweetness-and-light theology that would try to exclude him. On the other hand, I do not believe that God directly wills that we suffer tragedies and catastrophes but he, clearly, allows us to endure them and, sometimes, to be consumed by them.

Theology speaks of God's permissive will as opposed to his deliberative will. It means by this that he allows bad things to happen but does not deliberately engineer them. In this theology we can say that God did not will the Famine nor does he will the premature death of your child. Rather, he allows them to happen. But why? Apart from a miraculous intervention, God does not interfere in nature's laws or with a person's freedom to drink and drive and, appallingly, to kill your child. The burden is on us to respect the dynamics of nature and to respect the rules of the road. And there is also a burden on God to allow nature its laws and dynamics and to allow humans their freedom of choice, no matter how poor that choice may be. If he doesn't then he makes us his robots. I said that God does not interfere with nature's dynamics and people's freedom apart from a few exceptions. There are examples in the gospel stories of Jesus intervening in the laws of nature when he raised Lazarus from the dead for his distraught sisters and when he raised from the dead the only son of the poor widow of Naim.

I am trying to respect scripture and nature and human freedom in this treatment of our question about Famine and death. In doing so I see no particular reason to blame God for the Famine or to say that it was his punishment on our ancestors. I see no reason for saying that God wills the death of a child. But, clearly, he permits famine and death. The question can only be about God's permissive will. And that we do not fully understand. It is an ultimate question whose answer I suspect can only be found in the inner mind of God.

What I have written seems to contradict the way many parents think about the death of their child and God's role in it. You cannot walk around a cemetery without seeing such words as these on children's headstones: 'God took you from us' or 'God wanted another little angel in heaven so he chose you'. These words do not seem to reflect God's permissive will but his deliberate action in the death of the child. The words trouble the orthodox believer and they can haunt the sleep of the very young. I think there is more to them than meets the eye and maybe they express at least as much human psychology as theology. What might these words conceal and reveal?

Do they conceal the *real* truth, the truth that is cold and blind and unacceptable and useless to humans in their loss, that nature or human neglect or a medical mistake or a drunk driver actually did this and not God? Do they conceal the hurt of the mother who *really* wants to say: 'We so loved you but a cruel God took you from us'? Do they conceal the anger of the father who writes very different words in his heart, à la Yeats: 'Cast a cold eye on life, on death ... and on God'? Do they conceal the questioning and the grudge that some mothers and fathers and siblings will bring into their relationship with God for the rest of their lives?

Or do those words on the headstone reveal the ready acceptance that people of real faith have in their depths despite their awful loss? Do those words reveal a faith and a trust in God that is far deeper than my own and that has no need of distinctions between God's permissive will and his determinative will? Do those words profoundly signal that people of deep faith *do* actually understand that God's will is only permissive in their tragedy and that they endure a loss, in imitation of Jesus, that was brought about by others and not by the hand by God?

At the back of such words is, I believe, their abiding faith that a gentle God reaches down and picks up our deepest losses, those awful personal losses that are the broken and crushed pieces of a child or the cancered shadow of a loved parent, and gathers them into the warmth and life and wholeness of himself.

Mass bores me to death

Mass bores a lot of people. And it's not just young people. Some Masses bore even priests. Most bored of all may be the professional liturgists. These are the people who study the history of the Mass, how it is structured, what forms it has taken over the centuries, and how best it should be presented to people today as a critical part of their lives. The professional liturgists are the ones who hound parish priests about how boring their Masses are and what changes they must introduce to make them 'relevant.'

The day is gone when we got people to Mass by putting them under pain of mortal sin and damnation. I suppose that thinking belongs to a time when the best way of getting important things done in the church was to attach fear and penalties to them for non-compliance. Most institutions still operate that way. You only have to think about your job or your taxes or your mortgage or your TV licence. Default on these and you are penalised. But the church should rely on a different form of persuasion. After all, we are a voluntary organisation.

The church still has these penalties on the books but they do not impress most people today. Absence from Sunday Mass may result from the people's new and free way of looking at the Sunday Mass obligation. It may result, as observers say, from a weakening of the faith or because of the scandals. It may be due to modern sophistication or the spirit of the age. It may be due to more and more people taking personal responsibility for their relationship with God. But I think we must also include the observation of the liturgists that many people are absent from Mass because we are not paying enough attention to the ways it can be celebrated for different age groups and for different levels of interest.

Although the Mass has the elements of a great drama and is tailor-made for dramatic presentation, the way we have celebrated it for some centuries has been anything but dramatic and inspiring. It was presented, so the liturgists say, almost in silence with a priest mumbling Latin to a wall and his back to the people as though they didn't belong. Even now, with the changes, Mass seldom grabs people's attention except when some special occasion comes along. What's missing is the visual aspect mainly. In contrast, you notice that the pop singer surrounds himself or herself with back-up, audience participation, lights, sound, energy, vitality and visualness. The performance is a happening. It is an event. It is memorable.

Some of you may shiver at the comparison. I appreciate your shiver. It's not my style either but it does have its pointers and it helps answer our question as to why young people find Mass so boring. They come from this kind of experience of what a dramatic moment, an event or a happening should be, and their expectations for Mass are coloured with the same experiential brush.

Certainly, the Mass should be made more attractive for them in ways that are tuned to their experiences. There's nothing wrong about that. Haven't we used a parallel model for years with children's Masses here at home and with catechetical Masses in the mission fields? What about the Pope's 'big event' Masses with youth?

But I wouldn't want to give the impression that all the people who are bored with Mass are bored because of the lack of participation, drama, emotion, vitality, colour and visualness in the liturgy. Many will tell you that their problem with the Mass is quite different. They say they do not really understand the Mass, or why it's supposed to be so important for them, or how to get real meaning from it so that it touches their daily lives. They do not know why the bishops and priests expect their attendance as if this alone defined their faith and salvation. What they are raising here is the 'head' side of the question of why people are bored with Mass.

Some people are bored with Mass simply because they do not understand it and so cannot appreciate it. I think their difficulty is part of the wider and most critical matter before the church today: the need for adult catechesis for people who live in an educated and explanatory world. St Peter wrote that we are to 'give the reason for the hope' that we have in following Christ. (See 1 Pt 3:15) The church needs to give persuasive reasons for everything it asks the people to do in Christ's name, especially when it insists on the Mass and when it puts people under penalty to attend it.

So, why do I go to Mass? I'll speak for myself. Sheer habit is one reason. Sounds terrible? Actually, it's not a bad reason for starters. We were told in our catechism that every virtue is a habit. I'm so used to going to Mass that if I stopped I'd feel part of me had died. So, habit is one reason why I, and many others, go to Mass

I also go to Mass for reasons which are so fundamental that without them I believe I am not a Christian at all, just a pretend Christian. Let me try to explain that mouthful.

At the beginning of time, as the scripture has it, God worked for six days and on the seventh he ceased his work. Sabbath means the cessation of work. 'So God blessed the seventh day and hallowed it.' (Gen 2:3) The Sabbath became a day for praising God and for worshipping him. Central to the Sabbath is 'the calling of a sacred assembly,' i.e., calling the people to worship God as a community. (Lev 23:3)

At the beginning of our Christian faith, the apostles, of course, were Jews. They continued to worship in the temple but they also began celebrating 'the breaking of bread,' i.e., the eucharist. Gradually, the eucharist replaced the temple worship and Sunday replaced the Sabbath. Sunday became the Christian Sabbath day. It is the day Christ rose from the dead. These Jewish and early Christian factors determine why we go to Mass on Sundays.

But why the Mass as our form of Sabbath worship; why not something else? Again, we look to our Jewish ancestry. On the eve of the Jewish liberation from Egypt, God set the feast of Passover as a remembrance of the actual liberation event itself. The feast of Passover is a remembrance through worship. Jewish people celebrate the Passover in remembrance of the night God passed over the land of bondage, Egypt, and saved them through the sprinkling of the lamb's blood on their doors. He told them that they must re-enact the Passover in perpetuity as a worship remembrance once they entered the land of promise. (See Ex 12:21ff) The apostles regarded Jesus as the Passover lamb of the new covenant. The Sabbath and the Passover worship are key in Judaism. Sunday (as our Sabbath) and Jesus (as our Passover) are key in Christianity. They are separate events in Judaism; they are combined in our faith.

Jesus is the paschal lamb in whose blood we pass over from sin and darkness to grace and light. The Christian Passover, remembered and re-enacted in the worship form that we call the eucharist, is a far more potent Passover than the old one. The old Passover involved a small people passing over from bondage to freedom. The new Passover in Jesus is a passing over of multitudes of people in every generation from the kingdom of sin and Satan to the kingdom of grace and God. It spans all history and it embraces all the nations.

If I am a true Christian I am tied to these antecedents, to this spiritual ancestry, to these foundations. I cannot, with theological integrity, call myself a Christian believer or claim to be doing God's will if I ignore these core ingredients of the Christian life. They tell me what I ought to be doing every Sunday. A beautiful Mass, a wonderful liturgy that would highlight this marvellous story, would help me and so many others. But a boring one does not really hinder me personally because I know what I'm doing at Mass and why I'm there.

People sometimes say that they worship God better at home than in church at Mass. They find spiritual satisfaction just sitting at home, reflecting on the scriptures, listening to music, talking to God in private; or maybe meditating by the sea, or climbing the mountains God made, or just pottering about in the garden among the beauties of God's nature. They are perfectly right to seek God in these ways. God is found among them. They are all forms of worship and people do worship God through them. And he is probably more appreciative of these forms of worship than even they realise. But I don't think it should be an either/or thing – either these private forms of worship or joining with the community of believers in the public form of worship we call Mass. Our Lord asks for both in the gospels. Yet they are not equal and I have no doubt, judging from the centrality of the Last Supper in his life, which one the Lord himself prefers for us.

The most important reason I go Mass, and it is a reason of the heart as well as of the head, is this: I go because the Lord *commands* my presence. I go because the Lord himself – not the bishop or the priest or the mammy – invites me and even commands my participation. Mass is our word for the re-enactment of what Jesus did at the Last Supper. And we re-enact it because he commanded that we re-enact it in remembrance of him.

> He said to them: 'I have eagerly desired to eat this Passover with you before I suffer'.... Then he took a loaf of bread, and when he had given thanks, he broke it and gave it to them, saying, 'This is my body, which is given for you. *Do this in remembrance of me.*' And he did the same with the cup after supper, saying, 'This cup that is poured out for you is the new covenant in my blood.' (Lk 22:15, 19-20)

Matthew (in 26:26) has Jesus saying of the bread: 'Take, eat; this is my body.' Mark (in 14:22) also has the command about the bread: 'Take; this is my body.' St Paul has the command of Jesus about receiving both the bread and the cup and doing this in remembrance of him. (See 1 Cor 11:24-25)

I take Our Lord's words, 'Do this in memory of me,' as a command to his followers and, therefore, to you and me. It is a command that occurs just before his death. That makes it impossible to ignore. It is his final will and testament. Every time I attend Mass and eat his body and drink his blood I am fulfilling his command, his last wish, his will and his testament.

Gathered around him at this last meal are his most intimate followers. They are there by invitation. 'I have eagerly desired to eat this Passover with you.' (Lk 22:15) Every time I attend Mass I am there as an intimate of Jesus, a special friend. I am there by his invitation reaching me across the centuries.

What am I actually doing at Mass? I am involved in the re-enactment of the Lord's Supper, the making present at this moment in my parish church of what he made present in the upper room. I do it because he asked for it. What did he make present? He made present his body broken for us and his blood shed for us in the forms of bread and wine to be consumed by us.

It is critical to note that Mass is a re-enactment of what Jesus did at the Last Supper. It is not a memorial service in the modern sense. We are re-enacting what Jesus did and we are not just remembering it. Let me try to explain that.

In the Judeo-Christian view, a saving event is not something that happened long ago and then fossilised itself in history, as it were, so that we are now only able to have a commemoration ceremony about it. When a Jewish family in Dublin or New York celebrate Passover in the year 2001 they are not just doing a memorial service (as that expression is understood today) to something that happened long ago in their history: they are re-enacting the actual event. In this sense, the Passover event becomes as present and as potent for them today as it was at its first enactment in Moses' time.

In the same way, when we celebrate our Passover, the Mass, we are not just remembering something done two thousand years ago in the upper room. We are not just taking out an old video from 2000 years ago, as it were, and playing it every Sunday. We are making the original event present right now in this parish church in all its power and with its full measure of grace for us. We do not rely on ethereal waves or magic wands to receive the power and the grace that Christ won on Calvary. It is through the rites he commanded us to do that the graces of Calvary reach each new generation of Christians and us. Hence, the power and grace of the Mass.

It is the making present of the power and grace of Christ by means of the Mass and the sacraments, but especially the Mass, that made men as different in personality as Pope Pius XII and Fulton J. Sheen exclaim, 'It is the Mass that matters!' It is Jesus himself who has chosen the rituals by which his great graces reach us. And Mass is the central ritual. I, for one, will not presume it should be otherwise.

Those, then, are the reasons why I go to Mass. What I have tried to describe is the reality that seeks to be expressed in all the talk and argument about the old liturgy and the new liturgy. We can argue over how best to express it and what forms are most appropriate. The church tries to express it in Latin and in English, in the 'old' Mass and in the 'new' Mass, in a magnificent visual liturgy in a great cathedral and in a quiet simple Mass said in a room. There is no easy answer for the liturgists or for the parish priests or for the people to the question of how best to present the liturgy. But for the person who appreciates the magnificent reality behind the Mass, and the power-presence of Christ in it, there can never be a question of boredom no matter what the setting may be.

All the hypocrites in there

When someone talks about all the hypocrites in church one is tempted to give the riposte of the English vicar who said, 'We can always find room for one more.'

I think that despite the higher levels of education and democracy and wealth that modern society now enjoys it was never more crass in its speech and extreme in its judgements. Everyday language is peppered with blasphemy and foul words. We don't seem to be able to speak a normal language and the segregation and labelling of individuals and groups by the merchants of hate continues untouched by civil rights and sensitivity training.

If you impose pressure on the hate groups, they and their labelling and their segregationist mentality merely go underground for awhile. There is no real change of mind because there is no conversion of heart.

So, the English vicar's riposte is nothing less than the truth. The one who calls others hypocrites is one himself and possibly a bigger one. He is surely not at ease with life or God or himself.

I don't find the church full of hypocrites: I find it full of sinners like myself. A hypocrite is someone who fakes virtue. A sinner is someone who knows he doesn't have much virtue but would like to get some more. That's why so many of us are in church. We couldn't be in a better place given our condition.

Now the one who calls us hypocrites knows perfectly well what he's doing. He knows the difference between a hypocrite and a sinner but, true to the world he inhabits, he prefers to use an extremist label. He himself is usually someone who used to be in church and he remembers that Jesus loves sinners. But he won't call us sinners. That would not serve his purpose. He also remembers that Jesus lashed out at hypocrites and he'd like to believe he's on the high moral ground with God. Beneath this charade is a person very upset within himself and with the world and in that order.

The church is full of sinners because the church is made up of sinners. People and priests alike. That is not said casually. We sinners are aware of our condition. We accept the painful words of Joseph de Maistre: 'I do not know what the heart of a rascal may be; I know what is in the heart of an honest man; it is horrible.'[6]

The Irish generations have been generations of the peasant and the poor lining up for confession knowing their sinfulness, gathering in droves for the annual novena where horror of sin was central, striking their breasts with a thump and not a politeness at the words 'Lord, I am not worthy to receive you,' and receiving communion only weekly or monthly so great was the perceived distance between the holiness of God and their sinful selves. There was much wrong with this reticence but it surely pointed to the people's identification of themselves as poor sinners. God bless them, I believe they were saints.

When you look at old pictorials of the First World War you invariably find a photo of a dugout with *Dressing Station* written on it. I have one that shows a tent with *Casualties Here* on it. The tent is standard field issue, yet there's also a white arrow pointing to the slit door that any soldier would already be familiar with. I wondered at first why it needed a pointing arrow in addition to the casualty sign. Then I realised that the soldiers leading the men who were blinded in a gas attack would themselves be half-blind from the same attack. I like that image as an analogy for priests and people. Both are wounded. Even the healer is in need of healing.

I also love the realism Our Lord expressed in this passage about the kind of people he wants around him:

> When the scribes of the Pharisees saw that he was eating with sinners and tax collectors, they said to his disciples, 'Why does he eat with tax collectors and sinners?' When Jesus heard this, he said to them, 'Those who are well have no need of a physician, but those who are sick. I have come to call not the righteous but sinners.' (Mk 2: 16-17)

The church, taking its cue from Jesus, is in the sinner business. That's why it's full of them. The church is their hospital.

More than twenty years ago a sermon of mine was published on

'Wounded Healers'. The two words originated, I believe, with the late Fr Henri Nouwen and were becoming common usage at that time. Among other things I wrote:

> Children and people generally seem to expect far too much of their parents and clergy. They have the idea that any weakness on the part of parents or clergy is hypocrisy and therefore invalidates their authenticity. They forget that Jesus alone is called the sinless one in scripture and that we, his followers, are not greater than the Master. (See Mt 10:24) In many ways, we are responsible for our children's and our critics' attitude. We insist on covering up our own weaknesses and those of the church. Indeed our whole society is packaged to present its best face and its best profile. Nothing of sores and wounds must show in public. It's all so like a conspiracy to deny the existence of failure and the need for redemption.

So, the charge of hypocrisy was as current then as it is now. It is nothing new. The church no longer hides its weak human side. It never should have. The church is the epitome of the wounded healer. The church is always sublime on one level and deeply ragged on another. The church has Christ's healing face and the face of our wounded humanity. Neither of its faces is the face of the hypocrite. It generates saints but is always full of sinners. That's as it should be because the most fundamental gospel of all is the gospel that we are sinners in need of redemption.

The scourge of writers

The relationship between the church and Irish writers for much of the last century was a strained and a sad one. It is sometimes described as the clash of dogmatism with imagination. Being a theologian, it illustrates for me the failure of Irish theology to illuminate the relationship between Christ and the artistic imagination (specifically here, the literary imagination).

When Irish independence was achieved, the church found itself in a position of power and influence such as it never had in hundreds of years. The new Free State gave it its backing in return for the church's blessing. David Fitzpatrick writes:

> The hierarchy rapidly achieved Catholic supremacy in the Free State.... After their excommunication of all practising Irregulars in August 1922, the bishops were rewarded for their support by Cosgrave's insistence that all legislation with moral implication be submitted to church leaders for approval before its introduction in the Dáil. Cumann na nGaedheal and the church were at one in regarding the Free State as a Catholic rather than a pluralist society, a precept which went unchallenged by both the Labour Party and Fianna Fáil.[7]

The first written constitution, however, did not favour the church in any way. It did not even mention it or its moral code. Nor was the new government keen to do so in a statutory manner because it would have to rely in great measure on the religious minority in matters of finance, and on the minority's business and political links with Britain. Nor did it need to bolster the Catholic Church since the church's prominence was guaranteed by its sheer numbers in the new state.

The only significant potential Protestant opposition was isolated by the Boundary Commission in the North and it was in another state. The people of the Free State as a whole were not likely to oppose the mind of the church on anything since the church had been identified for some time now with Irish nationalism and its cultural aspirations. The stage was set for ideological conformity and moral uniformity. The church may have seen itself in the ideal situation. But to a student of history and of human nature it could hardly have been in a worse one.

The church's record from the foundation of the new state to the end of the century is distressing in many ways. Several factors that might have played a modifying role in the church's power and influence had not endured. The Ireland of the United Irishmen's vision was gone. It would have had no place for any undue influence of religion in its scheme of things. The North was gone, and with it went most of the ecumenical meaning of the tricolour flag that flew over the new state. Connolly was dead, and with him went the socialist workers' republic that would have modified all traditional social institutions including the church.

If the first years of the new state had been peaceful ones it might have seen to it that the church's power would be a moderated one. But the first years were turbulent ones with political instability, Irregular military attacks, and sabotage of the national infrastructure. It led to civil war. What resulted from the war was a bankrupt nation, more mourning and division, no foreign investment, and no money to resurrect bridges, buildings and farms. Murders, recriminations and bitterness continued for years after the war ended. As a consequence, maintaining the authority of the state developed into the major concern of the government and there was no debate that might circumscribe the church's power and influence in the new order. The church's great power and influence were determined instead by the swirl of events and the circumstance of omission.

By the late 1920s the government and the church were dominant in the nation. The two institutions, it might be fairly said, were pushed into each other's arms by events and circumstances. They would come to control all aspects of the nation's life in future years. Therein, I feel, lie many things, including the seeds of the present public criticism – dismissal in many instances – of the church and, not least, the saga of the Irish writer and his negative imagination.

The new state passed the Censorship of Publications Act in 1929. Though this was some years before De Valera's 1937 constitution and the 'special position' that constitution would give to the Catholic Church, the Act played into the hands of the church. Its chief effect seemed to be the protection of 'orthodox' theology and the banning of material that opposed the church's teachings on sex and birth control. An Appeal Board was set up in 1949 which brought a measure of common sense to the absurdities of the censors. It did not, however, prevent the censors banning books on the basis of a single 'unorthodox' thought or sentence – not even from interdicting copies of the Billings method of natural birth regulation that I sent from the US to a Galway GP, a book published by the archdiocese of Los Angeles with the imprimatur of Cardinal McIntyre. In 1967, perhaps because of the new economy and the growing national confidence and with the changes of Vatican II in the air, another Bill allowed for books to be unbanned after twelve years.

The Censorship Act of 1929 was, of course, an act of the state. But the hand of the church leadership was felt to be in it by the people generally and by the writers in particular. In addition, self-appointed impromptu censorship was practised all over the country by priests and school teachers, librarians and newsagents, religious groups and the overly pious. Again, the hand of church leadership was suspected.

The effects on the writers were many. In the new state the writers were at war with a controlling government and church. The temperament of writers is liberal, their energy creative, their focus social and critical, and their trade is by nature imaginative. On the other hand, the nature of authority is realistic, controlling and generally conservative. The writers came up against institutional authoritarianism, control and puritanism. Present too were economic depression, a later economic war with Britain, and – in the narrow sense – the widespread peasant mentality. The people generally were rural and poor with little education. None of this formed a basis for some terrible beauty to be born in the creative literature of the new Irish state.

Writers interpreted their odyssey of the next two generations as the struggle of David with Goliath and the irony of the church as the right arm of Goliath was not lost on them. Irish writing, for a good forty years of the life of the new state, is among other things a chronicle of the creative writers' anger at state and church and people over the rejection of their art, vision, their form of truth, and their social value. The writers were outsiders in their own home. Their feeling of internal exile was as bitter as the external exile into which some of them felt they were forced. They were pariahs created by puritans. This may be the major part of their negative imagination. In spite of it all, they endured and created great literature.

What is the negative imagination? Imagination is what we traditionally ascribe to writers. Negative imagination can mean the depressing stories and scenes a writer chooses to develop. It can mean the point-of-view the writer brings to his themes and characters in the philosophical sense, either by direct authorial comment or through his characters. It can be the 'disharmony of opposites', the writer's struggle for self-affirmation against the pressures of conformity. The Irish writer is not unique in this inner conflict. All of us endure it in one form or another. But, historically, it torments reformers and revolutionaries, saints and creative artists. In the case of our writers, there was no light at the end of their tunnel in the conforming landscape of state and church, stagnant economy and populist mores. Hence their generally negative imagination. And hence the belated adulation they now enjoy in the new open order of things.

Did the struggle against conformity which almost broke them also make them? To what degree were their successes forged by the frustration of their hammer on the intransigent anvil of state-church-people? Would they have been lesser or greater artists without it? Who knows?

The effects for the church were many – and negative. The church was seen (and experienced by the writers) as collusive in maintaining a status quo that depressed the human spirit; as narrow and authoritarian; as ignorant of art and the enemy of imagination; as anti-intellectual. The church lost the pastoral benefits it could have had from an openness to the writers and to their particular gift because their works reflected accurately – in my view – the social conditions and pastoral needs of the times. The church in Ireland lost the benefit of what Vatican II called the 'insights' for 'pastoral mission' that can be found in the arts and in literature. The council encouraged the arts and literature to give these insights to the church. It was as if the council were addressing the Irish situation and turning it on its head.

But there was no immediate change on the official Irish church level. Fr Peter Connolly of Maynooth was aware of the pastoral mistake of the Irish church, and its continuation despite Vatican II, when he wrote in 1965: 'Much closer to the specific values of literature is the claim that the theologians cannot afford to ignore the insight of the more challenging contemporary writers in so far as these act as symptoms and pointers to areas of stress in the human condition of our time.'[8] Sean O'Faolain was able to write, long after the council and with continuing regret, that 'In Ireland, today, priests and laity still rest at ease – with one qualification. Only one group is held at arms length, the writers.'[9] Vatican II was revolutionary in its attitudes. It was not revolutionary in theology as such. As a result, bishops went home believing, in good faith I presume, that nothing significant had happened, that there would be, as my own American bishop said, 'no change'.

If it was irony for the writers to see their struggle with the church as a modern incarnation of the David and Goliath story, with the church as the bad Goliath, it was all the more ironic that the writer's pastoral value was acknowledged by the council but still rejected in Ireland. We could push the irony further by suggesting that our Irish writers should have been recognised as having a charismatic function in the Irish church. Instead, the church ignored it. Or didn't understand the charismatic function.

Church charisms are free movements of the Spirit independent of the usual church structures, offices and sacraments. Karl Rahner says that they are 'not foreseen by the official organs of the church' and yet 'are always and everywhere to be expected, because ... they belong to the nature of the Church.'[10] The purpose of a charism, he tells us, is to make the church more visible and more credible as the People of God. Charisms 'confront' the church in a novel way, and unexpectedly. The confrontation is not for the purpose of destruction but for renewal and reform; a challenge and a call to get back to the spirit of the gospel.

One may assume that the person or persons with the charism

are believers located within the church. There is no pre-requirement that they be saints, only that they manifest a particular charism or impulse from the Spirit.

What we had in the Irish writers was a group of the baptised, located in the church as much as any other group or profession is located in the church. Almost all the writers in question were practising Catholics and most retained their links with the church despite the hammering they got. It was too much, of course, for some. Can we say that they were in confrontation with the church in the charismatic sense? They did not look for negative confrontation with the church leadership but for the right to exercise their God-given gift. That gift inevitably confronted all that was wrong with the mentality and in the behaviour of the church of their time.

They would have made the church more visible and more credible if their talent and gift had been acknowledged as the grace that it was, and if a listening rather than an imperious church had freed itself of that collusive power that the writers pointed out as something counter-Christian. They would have made the church more visible and more credible if their portrayal of the symptoms and the sins, the stresses and strains in Catholic Ireland was taken, not as a string of unmentionables, but as insight for the church's own pastoral mission and as a task for restructuring grace.

Has the church leadership learned anything from this sad saga? It would be tragic if all it learned was to disengage from controversial questions and groups and movements and be silent lest it be humbled again. But that seems to be the outcome. Once bitten, twice shy. It is the wrong outcome.

The bishops seem to have less and less to say by way of input and social dialogue in our new society. They appear to have reduced their social agenda to influencing just a few safe items like education and the pro-life issues, and to turning out pastorals and position papers that fail to reach the general public. If they are deliberately pursuing some new policy of disengagement they are making a pastoral mistake. They are only helping the not-so-friendly others shape the new Ireland.

The church, by definition, must be a challenging and an engaging agent in society and in the world. It just needs to learn the rules of engagement. That's one lesson from the sad saga of the writers.

The church and pomp

We've often heard it said of British royal functions, 'You have to hand it to the Brits – they know how to put on a show.' They ought to. They have centuries of practice at it. Especially royal weddings, funerals and coronations.

The military all over the world are good at it too. Everyone likes a marching band with all the troops in line and in step, arms swinging in unison and bayonets glinting equally in the sun. The Vatican also does things well. There is pageant and colour at papal installations – coronations the church used to call them – and even the Pope's pastoral visits are elaborately staged and full of formality and colour.

Where does the apparent need for all this pomp and circumstance come from? The small people of the earth are said to be responsible for much of it. It is true that people have always been known to love spectacles. They still do.

Now, leaders are aware of the people's love of spectacle and they use it to their advantage. 'Keep them happy with bread and circuses' is an age-old maxim among the world's movers and shakers. Keep the people happy with celebratory events – it keeps them in line and in our camp. There's a good measure of disrespect for ordinary people in this attitude. A weakness in our human nature is exploited by the captains and kings of the earth. By authority.

When authority parades itself in public it has a huge audience. People seem to be enthralled. I suppose they love the glamour and the glitz, the carnival air, the chance to attach themselves to the extraordinary and leave the cares of life aside for a while. And they are happy to let a few at the top set the scene for them, to lead the show, to entertain them and to dazzle their eyes as we see in everything from choreographed football matches to entertainment extravaganzas.

Leaders, royal *and* religious, love to dress up and to be different. People readily tolerate this for a simple reason: according to psychologists we all like to dress up. And our leaders dress up more than anyone else. There's a whole psychology to it. It's mostly a psychology of control exercised through impression. Control through impression is expressed in distinguishing forms of dress, deportment, accompaniment and language. Titles of address are important and marks of deference. They, too, are distinguishing marks. Distinguishing what or whom? Basically, distinguishing them from us. We are the crowd needing control; the sheep in need of shepherding; the fickle and the feeble who must not be left alone; 'the great unwashed' of the nineteenth century image who are 'born to be led.' (These are phrases from the age of imperialism. I didn't make them up!)

If we follow the psychologists in the matter then we may as well agree right now that there will never be a world entirely free of pomp and there never will be leaders, royal or religious, devoid of the need for the trappings of power and authority. Even the Americans, who consciously eschewed royalty and titles when setting up their social forms and who profess the equality of man, still manage 'The Honorable' for a member of Congress and 'Your Honor' for the judge. (It's their spelling, not mine!) And the old Soviet politburo? It distinguished its members through hand-made Zils, country dachas, Black Sea villas and private sports clubs from the proletariat for whom they were supposed to be the exemplars of the classless man.

The theology of Vatican II made an effort to lessen pomp and circumstance in the church. Some of the responses in line with this were trite, even comical. The Pope lost his triple tiara, his all-embracing symbol of religious, civil and heavenly jurisdiction. Cardinals lost several feet off their regal trains. Bishops lost pieces of their ordination regalia and many replaced their ornamental croziers with plain wooden staffs. American monsignors dropped the Right Reverend prefix to which they were entitled. Priests dropped lace from their albs.

The theology of Vatican II which attempts to moderate pomp and circumstance in the church is a wonderful one. It is not found in any one document. It's spread throughout many of them. And it's not so much a matter of admonitions and cautions as it is a consequence of how the church has redefined itself and its mission in our time.

In the theology of Vatican II, the church triumphant has become the pilgrim church. The aloof church has become the listening and learning church. The regal church has become the servant church. The heavily hierarchical church has become the communitarian church. The judgmental church has become the confessing church. The legal church has become the scriptural church. That is the new theology. Whether the church actually transforms itself through this theology only time will tell. Many of 'the changes' which we see and which we argue over are attempts to put this theology into practice, however well or poorly. People debate whether the Pope is pursuing this vision of church or attempting to by-pass it for his own autocratic vision. People debate whether the local bishop and parish have taken it to heart or merely pay lip-service to it, and whether the laity are being kept from it or have quietly rejected it themselves. Behind all of it is the struggle between the new vision of church and the old.

At the moment, I think an honest critique would suggest that the church has no intention of dropping all pomp and circumstance, that its own particular sense of humanity and tradition will not allow it, and that it never intended its new commitment to the poor to be a radical commitment to a poverty of pomp and circumstance for itself. The leadership will remain the leadership and the distinctions and the trappings will stay in place, even if tactfully muted. The night of pomp and circumstance, of distinctions and titles seems set to go on.

Therefore, observers today are left with the same questions for the church that past generations of sinners and saints had for the church in their own time and place. They have no expectation of a new state of things such as was demanded by radical critics and reformers of history. Those radicals wanted things turned totally upside down. They wanted a one-dimensional theology of impoverishment for the church, a model of church that never allows it to show its quiet satisfaction and its hope of triumph, a leadership decked out in rags, and a fixation with the poverty of the stable and the sparse straw of the manger. What is wanted today is less radical.

What is wanted is the church's better alignment with the lifestyle of its Founder who could say, 'The foxes have holes, and birds of the air have nests; but the Son of Man has nowhere to lay his head.' (Mt 8:20) Is there any good reason why the pomp and the titles should continue among Christians?

St Paul writes in Galatians: 'There does not exist among you Jew or Greek, slave or freeman, male or female. All are one in Christ Jesus.' (3:28) We, in the church, are one and equal in Christ because of the intention and the grace of God. We have different gifts and charisms and functions to perform in the church but pomp and the courtly titles of the world need not be used to sign them. Consequently, we find in scripture a general aversion to pomp and titles in the Christian community. Only the Lord matters. Titles of Christian consequence belong to him alone. All the rest of us are disciples and learners.

St Paul refers to himself simply as Paul. He calls believers 'brothers' and 'sisters'. He uses the term 'Excellency' in one letter in an attempt to ingratiate himself with the addressee on behalf of the runaway slave, Onesimus. I don't doubt that Paul gave the civil authorities whatever titles their rank required. But that was a requirement in civil matters. In the church community, Paul did not use titles and I have no doubt he would be shocked at the rash of titles we use in the church today.

Take the clergy. Here are some titles officially in use: Father, Reverend, Very Reverend, Right Reverend, Most Reverend, Your Excellency, Your Lordship, Your Grace, Your Eminence, Your Holiness. Do we honestly think this syndrome reflects the absence of titles in Pauline theology or the spirit of discipleship expressed by the Lord in the following lesson?:

> James and John, the sons of Zebedee, came forward to him and said to him, 'Teacher, we want you to do for us whatever we ask of you.' And he said to them, 'What is it you want me to do for you?' And they said to him, 'Grant us to sit, one at your right hand and one at your left, in your glory.' But Jesus said to them, 'You do not know what you are asking. Are you able to drink the cup that I drink, or be baptised with the baptism that I am baptised with?' They replied, 'We are able.' Then Jesus said to them, 'The cup that I drink you will drink; and with the baptism

with which I am baptised, you will be baptised; but to sit at my right hand or at my left is not mine to grant, but it is for those for whom it has been prepared.' When the ten heard this, they became angry with James and John. So Jesus called them and said to them: 'You know that among the Gentiles those whom they recognise as their rulers lord it over them; their great ones are tyrants over them. But it is not so among you; but whoever wishes to become great among you must be your servant, and whoever wishes to be first among you must be slave of all. For the Son of Man came not to be served but to serve, and to give his life a ransom for many.' (Mk 10:35-45)

There is a valid distinction, of course, between clergy and laity in the church community. No one denies that. It is supposed to be a distinction of office or function, not of worth and equality. But the pomp and the titles suggest greater worth and inequality. And they continue to separate laity from clergy in too distinct a manner and only reinforce the pedestal view of the clergy. As long as there is too great a distinction between laity and clergy, underpinned by the syndrome of ascending titles, the clergy will rank higher than the laity in the community's consciousness, and not only in rank but in expectation of greater theological expertise and holiness. Thus, the two-tiered Christianity of the church is maintained and theology, whether of Paul or Vatican II, is neutralised.

These titles and trappings of Renaissance grandeur are inappropriate for a church now located in a world that is more and more democratic and that has itself developed simpler modes of address for honouring its leaders and heroes. In America, they always look to their ancestry. They find that their forebears fled Europe in order to get away from kings and princes and landed archbishops and other titled constraints so that they might fashion a more just and equal society in which they could worship the Lord with gospel simplicity. And they did it in a wilderness, as Israel of old was fashioned in the wilderness.

There is, for want of a better word, a kind of shadow in the titles business. There is a shadow in the sense that titles hide the person that is the priest and the bishop from the people, and in the sense that titles obscure Christ in all of them. Several times in the church's official documents and in the writings of the Pope, priests and bishops are told that the people must be easily able to see Christ in them. The same writings say that the people are to find their 'brother' and their 'fellow pilgrim' in the priest and bishop. It is difficult for the lay person to find Christ or his/her Christian equality with a 'brother in Christ' in the clergy when the conversation moves unequally between John/Mary/my child on the one side and Your Lordship/Your Grace/Your Eminence on the other.

We could put this titles versus Christian simplicity and equality issue in a box labelled 'unresolved tensions in the present church' and leave it at that. But that's precisely the trouble with the contemporary church. There are too many 'unresolved tensions.' All kinds of good things have been announced by church and the council and then left there, unconnected. There is no follow through. And again, so much is being affirmed in our time, without spelling out the consequences, that old and new visions co-exist in comfort, priorities are too many and too equal, and paradoxes and apparent contradictions appear. So much has been affirmed in our time, for example about clergy and laity, about common priesthood and ministerial priesthood, about baptism and ordination, about the Christed Christian lay person and the Other Christ priest, that little actually changes. The church in practice lives by many visions and many theologies. It also lives by disconnection. They are used to justify anything new or anything old that we wish to promote on the one hand or attack on the other.

The present Pope had the opportunity of ending the nightmare of titles by relinquishing some of his own. But he passed it by. In a response to the journalist Vittorio Messori, he wrote: 'Have no fear when people call me "the Vicar of Christ", when they say to me "Holy Father" or "Your Holiness", or use titles similar to these, which seem even inimical to the gospel ... These expressions ... have evolved out of a long tradition, becoming part of common usage.'[11] The Pope states that these titles 'are not important'. What is important, he says, is being 'a witness to Christ'. Why, then, not drop some of the official and personal titles? The Pope's official titles alone cover a half-page in Pope Paul VI's promulgation decree of the council documents! Why not drop them in favour of the evangelical description of the first Pope as simply Peter? It's the name Christ gave him.

In addition to acknowledging the pastoral drawbacks attached to some of his titles – but choosing not to do anything about them – the Pope acknowledged that his office, as it is understood in the Catholic Church, stands in the way of Christian unity. The history and theology surrounding the Petrine office is a matter for the experts. We will leave that to them. But it might help the cause of Christian unity a little, from the psychological standpoint, if the Pope let go of some of his more absolutist titles since, as he says, titles are unimportant. Again, things are said but the connections are not made.

By way of contrast, Gandhi wrote in 1925: 'In the majority of cases, addresses (i.e. titles) presented to me contain adjectives which I am ill able to carry. They unnecessarily humiliate me for I have to confess I do not deserve them.'[12] The title 'Mahatma' or 'Holiness' bothered him. He wrote in 1927: 'The Mahatma I must leave to his fate. Though a non-co-operator I shall gladly subscribe to a [parliamentary] bill to make it criminal for anybody to call me Mahatma.'[13]

It is all the more fitting that the followers of Jesus reflect a similar sentiment in regard to titles. But they do not. And so, the titles persist. The shadowing of Christ in the fog of titles will be with us in the church for as far into the future as one may see.

Why not? À la carte Catholicism

À la carte Catholics are people who want to remain in the church but who do not subscribe to some of its teachings. In other words, there are bits missing in their version of the Catholic faith. The missing bits are said to be the hard bits like birth control. They themselves would say they are the silly bits. On the other side of the Atlantic, Catholics who have bits missing from their faith are called cafeteria Catholics. They are like people in a cafeteria who select only the dishes they like from the huge menu. They select only the appetising dishes.

I realise that à la carte Catholics have a bad press not only with Rome and the bishops but even with parish clergy generally. They are viewed as people who are in the business of setting up a parallel church under the guidance of their own spirit (lower case 's') and with their own magisterium; an enterprise of considerable pride and fallacy. Hence, the term à la carte carries a negative connotation and is a derisory epithet among the clergy generally. From a pastoral point of view, I think we should read this whole scene differently.

There are many Catholics in the à la carte category. Some observers think they may be the majority in the present-day church. Obviously, the Pope and the bishops are upset. They want Catholics to accept and to practise what is called the full faith.

Condemnation of such Catholics will not address the pastoral challenge that they represent for the church. Now and then they are urged to live the full gospel and the whole Christian lifestyle. So far, I believe, they have not been challenged in a manner that could be called pastorally persuasive in tone or content and that might get them to change their ways. I have not seen an exercise of church leadership – and this is a matter of catechetical leadership – that tells them what the 'full faith' is or the full gospel or what the whole Christian lifestyle is supposed to consist of.

I mentioned this at a clergy dinner one day and the bishop said: 'It's all there in the *Catechism of the Catholic Church*. If they want to know what the full gospel is they can read that. They're well able to read blockbuster novels.' Now, the *Catechism* is 700 pages long. Some of it is in small print. On normal type it might spread itself over 800 pages. Does the bishop seriously believe that most people are going to curl up on a winter's evening with 800 pages of theology? Theology of its very nature does not flow like a novel! Is he not aware that even seminarians cannot cruise through the *Catechism* as though every page were self-explanatory? But it's the bishop's pastoral attitude more than the length of the book that is troublesome. It is rather like the remark of a young priest who said, 'If they won't come to church, that's their problem, not mine.' Such responses will not do anymore.

Christians in Ireland, just as around the world today, have very differing understandings of what the terms 'full gospel' and 'whole Christian lifestyle' and the 'full faith' and 'following Jesus' mean. Is our church leadership talking about birth control and blind obedience when it suggests that the à la carte Catholics are not living the full faith? Or are they talking about casual sex? Or missing some Sunday Masses? Or clubbing and pubbing with the Celtic Tiger? Or not going to confession? Or 800 pages of theology? It would help if everyone knew the answer.

Let's say the answer is something like this: The church does not want Catholics to make themselves, rather than the official church, the judge of how they should conduct their lives and what their faith should consist of. If they make themselves the judge of their own faith, are they not being a bit Protestant and democratic and self-reliant? I suppose they are. And, as I see it, they are right; because what they are doing is in harmony with Catholic theology whether traditional or post-Vatican II. It is in harmony with Vatican II's *Declaration on Religious Liberty* (1965): 'All are bound to follow their conscience faithfully ... the individual must not be forced to act against conscience nor prevented from acting according to conscience.' (#3) We must live according to our best conscience when all is said and done. That's where God's judgement on us is.

I try to live according to my best conscience. At least I believe I do. That conscience obliges me to accept my faith as best I understand it. I believe my personal faith coincides with what is understood as the full Catholic faith. Someone else's best conscience may not lead him or her to the same point. Maybe it will at a later stage in life.

I may not be like the à la carte Catholic in the content of my faith but I am very much like him and her in the process by which I believe in the content I subscribe to. This is my own situation in faith: Leaving aside the mystery of God's grace and looking at myself as theology defines me – a free acting agent responsible in conscience for my actions – I find the following:

I am a born Catholic but I remain one because I believe I should be, and I choose to accept that belief. I am a priest and I remain one because I believe that I should be. I subscribe to the teachings of the church and to the church's teaching authority because my lifelong study directs me to that acceptance. I do all of this because my conscience mandates it for me. What I have gone through, with God's grace, is a process involving *my* intellect, *my* personal freedom, *my* personal choice and *my* willingness of response. In other words, I looked at the menu and considered it and I found I wanted the whole thing. It was my choice and my decision and not an external imposition of the church. And God, according to the traditional and classical Catholic theology, doesn't want it to be any other way. I and the à la carte Catholic use the same *process* in accepting what we believe in but come to different conclusions.

Therefore, I'm jaundiced towards any easy condemnations thrown at the à la carte Catholics. Instead, I believe that the weight of criticism should be levelled at those who do the condemning. Where is the enlightening church? Where is the dialoguing church? Where is the calibre of reasoning and persuasion that everyone else uses, from health experts to insurance salespeople, to sell their product in this day and age?

The new Ireland, like the world, is a marketplace. The church has to enter the marketplace and compete by the rules of the marketplace. Nothing will fall automatically anymore into the church's lap. That's one thing the present Pope, with his endless pastoral visits, has always appreciated. He's out there teaching all the time.

If the local church wants cafeteria Catholics to practise the 'full faith' and to live the 'whole Christian lifestyle' it has to get out there and tell them what it is that it's talking about. Local churches had better learn how to process with people. They had better start competing intelligently in the free marketplace of ideas and ideologies and engage this generation with something of the tireless and intelligent persuasion of St Paul.

There is a phrase in Vatican II that was highlighted by the council fathers and that has become a critical pastoral axiom. It is this. In its pastoral mission the church must read the 'signs of the times' and respond accordingly. It must use the insights and expertise of the sciences. Now, one of those sciences, sociology, makes it clear that our present society is in process. It is fluid, economically driven, well-educated, developing a pluralistic form, encouraging religion into the shadows as a purely private matter, and open to European cultural standards and their secularising values. The middle and young generations have the same characteristics and personal values that we see generally in the western world. The chief one is independence of thought and action.

In this context, the church is not dealing so much with a doctrinaire form of Protestantism erupting within the fold, nor with a new form of heresy in the proper sense of that term, nor with a callous disobedience and disrespect, but with a differently constituted person. The person in the pews today, and the person the church would like to have back in the pews, is not a recyclable version of his or her all-accepting grandparents but one who is distinguished by self-determination and independence of action. The old methods of pastorality that were admonitions, threats, condemnations, off-the-cuff analysis and forced-fed content without the right to raise a question and receive a dialogical answer, are not only useless catechetical tools to such a person: they are meaningless.

Therefore, the à la carte Catholic is not simply a disobedient, selfish, churlish non-conformist. He or she is the person that has emerged from centuries of thought and social trial and error, and who has been fashioned from the best insights of philosophy and religion – including our own. That is where the à la carte Catholic has come from. We should have expected him and her and prepared our ministry for them. But, of course, we didn't. We are not a pro-active church.

The à la carte phenomenon has parallels in all the members of the church who are known as 'good Catholics' but the official church does not make an issue of these parallels. One parallel is broadly philosophical, the other psychological. Let me illustrate the first one. Let's say the church set 100 questions before me right now. They are all questions relating to Catholic doctrine and morals, to the 'full faith' and to the 'whole Christian lifestyle'. I am a trained theologian. I've spent my life in Catholic preaching and teaching. Yet, I am confident that I would not get a 100% grade. If the same exam were set to any priest or bishop I am confident the result would be the same. Are we therefore in the same boat with the à la carte Catholic? After all, we have bits missing. The church would say no. If we are not, then the issue with the church is not our ignorance of the 'full faith' but the fact that we are not deliberately choosing to ignore any part of it. The à la carte Catholic is. So, disobedience to the authority of the church is the real issue, so far as the church is concerned. But is that the real issue with God and is it the real issue for religion's emptying pews today?

Here is the second parallel. It concerns how we humans understand or grasp truth; how and why we select or reject, emphasise or moderate all our experiences and all our perceptions including the revealed truth of God and his church. There may be over 1000 structured forms of Christianity in the world today, a thousand sects that try to live the faith as they understand it. In some ways their faith is the same but in other ways it is quite different. Most, I suspect, would never dream of leaving their own for another. They believe that their take on the faith is the best and the most accurate understanding of it. Personal temperament has a lot to do with this, of course. Ten witnesses can see the same car crash and report it in conflicting ways.

Another example. There is the manner in which Vatican II has been reported and understood for the past nearly forty years. My own bishop stepped off the plane in 1965 at the end of the council and said to the assembled media, 'Two words – no change.' Ever since then we have been living with change.

Where does the à la carte Catholic fit into this? Well, the popular words that are used to describe this psychological phenomenon are 'filtering' and 'mindset.' Every teacher has the experience of trying to impart a piece of information only to see the student sift and strain it until little remains – or something entirely different emerges. Teachers of my childhood had the experience of giving a student an expert's analysis of, say, the Irish civil war or Irish neutrality during the Emergency, only to find that the student was already locked in the immovable mindset of his or her parents and grandparents on these questions. The à la carte Catholic, like all the rest of us, has a prior mindset and a filtering system that selects and prioritises, and that sometimes moderates or rejects.

If the church is serious about the à la carte Catholic it can begin by accepting the fact that, in terms of comprehensive religious knowledge and the 'full faith', the à la carte Catholic is not any different from the rest of the believers in church. A really comprehensive knowledge of the faith is lacking all over the place. If the church wishes to change things and to better inform the conscience of the à la carte Catholic and increase the religious knowledge of just about all the rest of us, then adult religious education offers a promising process, even if it is not an automatic guarantee of success. If the church wishes to penetrate the psychology of mindset and filtering, patience and persuasion will help. For sure, easy condemnations do nothing for the à la carte Catholic. Neither does the continuing catechetical silence that Catholic adults have had to endure for the generation and more since the end of the council.

What's wrong with partners?

The first thing that's right with 'partners' is the honesty of the word. It signals those who live as husband and wife without benefit, or bother, of a wedding ceremony.

Some are in a partnership because the first marriage failed and they can't get an annulment. Some are in a partnership because there are personal, economic or legal reasons why they don't wish to have a prior union nullified. Some are in a partnership because they can't be bothered to formalise things. Some are in a partnership because they don't believe it's anyone else's business to approve of their love by giving them a piece of legal paper. And some are in a partnership because they are trialling their relationship, with marriage as their future if they find themselves compatible.

There are many reasons why one should be reluctant to comment on an individual's personal relationships, especially those of an intimate nature. In our haste to do so, and to have everything right 'by the book', we forget that partnerships are older than the two agencies that claim some right to regulate them – the state and the church. We can also usefully remember that many modern states recognise partnerships as real marriages. And we can keep in mind that the basis of any state or church wedding is the exclusive partnership that already exists between two consenting individuals.

Having said that, I am quite conscious of the regulatory rights of the state as the agent of society and legislator of the people's will. There are legal, economic, social and welfare concerns attached to partnership and marriage that make these unions more than just the couple's private business. But what of the church? The church's regulatory laws only concern its own members. For its own members, it regards partnerships and 'trial' marriages as immoral. Why? The answer is in the Christian theology of marriage that we developed in the chapter 'Annulments: How can they?'

I think that the two most common forms of partnership today are these: There is the partnership of living together for reasons of sex and convenience and because it's the done thing today. Marriage is not in its purview at all. And there is the partnership in which the couple say they are testing their compatibility as possible marriage partners. The first of these is plain shacking-up or 'fornication' as the bible puts it. The second is taken seriously. It is called 'trial marriage.'

Marriage is a huge commitment. It is a sacrament. More and more marriages are breaking up. Christian marriage is a permanent state. It is not easy to get an annulment after going through a sacramental marriage. Annulment is a legal process. It opens old wounds. People suffering and under stress from a broken marriage may not wish to re-visit it for a long time. There still is a stigma attached to the broken marriage in many communities. There can be a question about one's maturity or fidelity. There can even be a rider or a caveat in the decree of annulment about one's suitability to enter another marriage. These are all reasons why some couples enter trial arrangements.

Sacramental marriage is a life-long commitment. But we live in an age of short-term commitments. People change their jobs and their homes and their clothes and even their faces at a rate unheard of in the past. Change defines modern life. Permanence is something that has the aura of the past or of eternity about it. The whole social scene puts a question mark in front of anything with the word 'permanent' attached to it. All of these considerations make the modern couple think twice. They make them easy targets for entering a partnership as a trial for marriage.

Yet, those who are set on trial marriages need to consider the other side of the coin. There are a few sobering observations to be made about trial marriages. First of all, it's not in the Christian scheme of things. That is the primary consideration for any follower of the Lord. Secondly, any survey I've seen in recent years shows no better rate of success for trial marriage over traditional marriage. In fact, the very first survey I read in the American *Family Co-ordinator* (vol 28, n 1) back in 1979 showed that trial marriage was slightly less successful than traditional marriage in keeping couples together. Thirdly, a couple will not discover their compatibility for marriage by a trial run. Let me elaborate on that point a little.

In our lives we go through stages of development and growth and times of crisis. A trial couple would have to stay together for a lifetime to be sure of compatibility through all of life's passages. And a trial is just that – a trial. It lacks the up-front commitment for life to love and cherish, for better or worse, this one person. It is a provisional thing based on the premise: Let's see if we get on well together for a few years and if we do we will make it permanent. In this sense, a trial marriage is never a valid trial of the real thing. It is a fiction.

I wrote the following many years ago on the subject of trial marriages. Perhaps it has something useful to say to all who are in partnerships whether of the trial or the hang-loose kind. It is a reflection on human psychology and not a sermon:

> What may be the most practical consideration of all is this: can the trial situation give adequate expression to what a man and a woman do for each other, with each other, and to each other when they decide to draw a circle about themselves? I do not believe the trial situation can cope with the dynamics of personality that are activated when persons enter this closed circle. In crucial ways, the core person and the whole person become active, and the dynamics of these centres of self cannot be satisfied by arrangements and trials but only by a union which supports those psychological intensities that is total, fully committed, fully surrendering of self, and permanent.
>
> I disagree with those who feel that the dimensions of marriage we call 'exclusive love', 'union of hearts', and 'permanence of duration' originate in the needs of society, in the needs of child-rearing, and in the needs of social law and order. I believe these dimensions express deep yearnings in the core of the human person and have their origin there.[14]

Prods and Papists and Jesus

The troubles in the North were an awful religious spectacle to the world. Much as many of us who lived abroad tried to persuade people that it was really a matter of politics and economics rather than of religion, I don't think we had any converts. There were, instead, some who dropped religion altogether, at least the mainline Catholic and Protestant versions. In any event, Jesus lost.

Were we just fooling ourselves when we told people that religion was only accidentally involved; that the religious divide only happened to coincide with the all-important political and economic lines? I still think religion is not the nub of the matter. Maybe the potential Christian converts we lost actually understood this. Maybe what really turned them away was something else. Maybe it was watching their television set as it unfolded primitivism in the shape of the triumph of religious tribalism and hate over democracy and decency. The form of Christianity that was on display was simply awful to them.

Religious symbols were everywhere on display in the North and great damage was done to the cause of religion. God was dragged into the heart of things and one wondered if even he understood the convolutions of this politicised religious mayhem. A peace activist put the knife in things when she said, 'I wish to God there were no Protestants and Catholics in that place, only *human* beings.'

Now those are controversial words. And arguments could be raised in opposition to them. Sadly, arguments can be made in support of them as well. I'm not interested in those arguments here. I'm interested in looking at the sort of Jesus that the North presented to the world. I am interested in the damage done to a wonderful side of Ireland – its Christian missionary tradition. Even if we consider only the Irish missionary tradition since the Reformation, that tradition is a rich and vibrant one. It involves both Catholic and Protestant efforts for Christ. We see the missionary fruits of the Scots-Irish Presbyterians and of the Irish Catholics in places as diverse as North America and Korea.

Very, very long before either the modern missionary effort or the Reformation, there was practically a unity of identification between the Scots and the Irish. It was seen in the monasteries of Derry and Iona, in Columba and Aidan, in their combined missionary work among the peoples of north Britain for the sake of the gospel. The two peoples, although going separate ways since the Reformation and becoming instead the 'two traditions,' have long been the Celtic missioner for Christ to an unenlightened world. Celtic unity is the oldest identity of both traditions. Christianity is a close second. But has walking in separate ways, and growing more and more apart in Christ – such an irony in itself – for the past three-and-a-half centuries, finally caught up with them? What a shame that an observer of our time would say of the North, 'I wish to God there were no Catholics and Protestants in that place, only human beings.' In other words: Does the long-time missionary now need to be missioned to? Has the North not itself become chronically unenlightened in Christian terms?

The religion we saw on display in the North brings up again the issue of the pastoral effectiveness of the churches. The sort of God that the world saw in the North is opposed to the real God revealed to us by Jesus. And it raises an even more challenging question for all the churches: Can religion really reach the roots of people and transform them? A test case for our time is the North. Does the North say no? Is that the *theological* meaning of the events of the past thirty years?

The television images showed us a God in warpaint. For one side, God was the Warrior God of the Old Testament, the primitive, purging and ethnic cleansing God whose single item agenda was to displace an unworthy people in favour of 'his own' (Jn 13:1) and to bend their rebelliousness and stubbornness (See Deut 31:27) to the God-ordained social order. Attempts were made by various politicians and spokespersons on that side to moderate the American TV images. They insisted that the only demands anyone was making of the minority were the normal democratic and civil ones: acceptance of the legitimate state and of the rule of law and order.

On the other side, God was the God displaced from his temple in Jerusalem. He was the God exiled with his humble people to the waters of Babylon. There, the impoverished people 'sat and wept ... On the aspens of that land we hung up our harps.' (Ps 137:1-2) They sang no alleluias or hallelujahs, only the dirges of death and martyrdom. Both groups gave us a reduced version of the real God. Military people do this all the time. Patton and Montgomery are classic examples. Both were God-fearing men. Both were agile in quoting scripture (that is, the passages that suited them). But theirs was a very truncated God. Before his greatest triumph, Alemein, Montgomery dismissed a chaplain for preaching a sermon that was not geared to the clash of arms and 'the Lord mighty in battle.' (Ps 24:8) Patton promoted a chaplain whose prayer got him good weather for the Battle of the Bulge. Their God was only the Warrior God. Their understanding of God stopped in the middle of the Old Testament.

Some people seem to have no trouble in redefining God to fit their hearts, their hurt and the situation at hand. All of us, of course, tend to give God the shape that we believe fits our personal need and this can be a valid use of scripture insofar as the revealed God is there to comfort us as well as to challenge us. So giving God our own shape is something we all tend to do in times of need. However, the shape we give God in our need must never be so enlarged or so reduced that the real God is redefined and becomes only the measure of our particular need or the situation at hand. That is what happened to the real God throughout the troubles. He was never allowed the progressive unfolding he is given in scripture. He was never allowed to become the Abba-Father that he is, or the full definition of God that he became in the face and heart of Jesus. 'He is the reflection of God's glory and the exact imprint of God's very being.' (Heb 1:3) What the North did with God, and what the generals do with him, is called reductionism. God was seriously reduced in the North because God was chronically politicised in the North.

The God the world saw was the kind of God (and the kind of

Jesus and the kind of religion) that no one with decency or intelligence is willing to accept. The Protestant portrayals may have been the more significant and the more damaging to the cause of God. They were more significant in that they were the more visible and the more frequently touted, and in that religion and politics appeared knitted fast in the majority's mentality. They appeared everywhere: on banners, walls, arches, gable ends; in speeches, rallies and remembrances. 'For God and Ulster.' 'For God and Country.' 'For God and Queen.' 'Ulster: Faithful and True.' These last words properly apply to the triumphant Christ in Revelation 19:11 who rides a white horse. One notes that the triumphant William of Orange also rides a white horse on the Orange Order banners. And so on ... all the paraphernalia that is the legacy of the Williamite wars and of the Cromwellian wars with their theology of providential Protestant destiny; and of Carson's threat of war with his covenant signed in blood, so deliberately reminiscent of the blood sacrifices between God and his people in the scriptures. It is a theological mentality that almost never moves beyond the first books of the Old Testament. And it deliberately does not move beyond it. For to advance forward in the scriptures does not suit the situation, the history or the ideal. Such an advance would, theologically speaking, attack the present order and collapse its future.

The Catholic portrayals of God were few. They were not on banners, walls or in rallies and speeches. They appeared at funerals, and then only as the conjunction of the hooded men firing their volley over the coffin with the crucified Lord of love on it. The gun and Semtex, not God and religion, are the war symbols of the minority insofar as the minority is represented by the Republican element. The reason why the Catholic portrayals of God were few is simple enough. Religion does not invest Republicanism the way it invests Unionism and Loyalism. In fact, religion is not a component of doctrinaire Republican philosophy at all. It never was.

There was in the North an apparent failure of religion. Did the failure point to a flaw in the nature of religion itself that prevents religion from getting at the roots of people and transforming them, or is it an external limitation due, perhaps, to religious ignorance and to the deliberate theological reductionism of the various religious and political leaderships?

The outside world once again saw religion as a danger and it wondered if religion should have any place in an enlightened society. The North was the same old noxious religious tape being played all over again: Protestant versus Catholic, Gentile versus Jew, Muslim versus Christian, Hindu versus Muslim. The young generation had every reason to believe, as many international experts believe, that a new world order must not only not provide for religion but actively suppress it. The world imagined by the young during the troubles was not the world envisioned by Presbyterian John Knox or by Catholic Vatican II but very much the world of the Beatles' *Imagine.* It was a world without war and without hate 'and no religion too'.

But history rescues Christianity from its contradiction in the North and from the Beatles' philosophy of achieving a better world by dumping religion. History records the lives of Christian people who took the religious enterprise seriously and fully. For them there was never a question of reducing the range of God or of Christ or scripture and grace. The result was seen in individual saints, and in communities, and in societies. They proved that the words of St Paul were no empty Christian ideal and that people can be changed and reconstructed by gospel and grace. 'So if anyone is in Christ, there is a new creation.' (2 Cor 5:17) History records the admiration of the pagans who said of the early Christians, 'See these Christians: how they love one another!' (a phrase attributed to Tertullian). History also shows that a contemporary country, the Netherlands, homeland of William of Orange himself, with a mix of Catholics and Protestants, can progress politically, socially and economically. The 'two traditions' in Holland had lived for generations in tension and in competition with each other but without violence. Now they are living together in active tolerance and with ecumenical support for each other because they recognise their common roots in the Lord Jesus. It could be done. It was and is being done. So, why not in the North?

The century ended with the missionary finally being missioned unto. The missionaries came from London and Dublin and Washington. They carried mobiles and briefcases and fax machines. Governments and trading blocks were behind them. They were serious and they were determined. The North was an embarrassment, even a scandal, to the first world.

There were other missionaries too. These were of the feedback variety. The TV images upset expatriates all over the world in a beneficial way. The length of the troubles allowed expatriates to progress from narrow sectarian support of the two camps back home to a desire for a settlement once and for all. The British crown was embarrassed by the jingoism of loyalism that belonged to the triumphalism of the long-departed Victorian age. The plain people of Britain showed no particular feeling of union with the Scots-Irish nor with the political biblicism that belonged to a century earlier. Devolution and assembly were on their agenda for even they had outgrown Swinburne's view of the union as a sacred thing that 'heaven hath done.' The North was caught in a time warp. It would have to be extricated from the outside.

The European Union saw in the mirror of the North the reflection of a European history it hoped was dead and buried. More than one representative of the secularised and somewhat pagan first world asked, ironically, if the North was an ethical place to do business in. The wisdom of the world had finally concluded that the North, as a most unusual quasi-state, with no prior model and no recognisable blueprint for its future, was never a viable proposition. It was built on a political earthquake fault. It was always a bridge too far.

The Good Friday agreement arrived courtesy, I suppose, of all of these influences. But I would like to think that there was another and quite determinative influence, and I think that the later referenda votes give credence to it. The people of the North themselves, even before the agreement took its first step, had begun to speak with feeling of the need to end the war and the violence, the sectarianism and the downward spiral. They had already begun to talk of settlement and of a series of genuinely democratic structures. I want to think that it was not the futility of the war, nor the constant weeping of the mothers in this modern Ramah, nor the secular missionaries that shaped the change of heart. I realise full well that these were all contributors in their way and that theology calls them natural graces.

I want to think that on both sides the grace of God broke through. I want to think that the two traditions realised that the men and women of violence and the demagogues had ruled for too long and that the ideals, however confused, that had once marked the two traditions were now abused horribly. I want to think that the vast majority in both traditions reached down into the roots of themselves, and into their deepest heart, and found the Lord Jesus already there with an invitation they could not refuse.

Sanitising Ireland

When one talks about sanitising Ireland one is not, unfortunately, talking about cleaning up the litter which disfigures God's lovely landscape here. Nor is one talking about eliminating the dirty little brown envelopes that signal dirty political pockets. Nor is one talking about washing the unlaundered consciences that launder dirty money of all kinds. One is talking about the invention of a new Irish society at the expense of far too much of the old.

Someone's reshaping Irish society. That's nothing sinister in itself. Society is not something that is born and develops through some law of nature or the hand of fate. It does not appear out of thin air or from the hand of God pre-assembled. It is fashioned by human beings. Contemporary societies, including our own, are planned constructs. They are the concretisation of someone's vision and the result of someone's fashioning. Some cultural aspects of a society may resist planning, control and manipulation and a society may seem firmly set in its constitution, laws and traditions, yet it is a living and a changing thing because, as the Americans say, it is a people thing.

In our lifetime, we have seen Ireland change from Free State and commonwealth to independent republic. There have been major changes in the constitution, even three different constitutions, and many changes in the law. Traditions, customs and mores have changed too. None of this happened by accident. External events and external influences caused some changes; internal need and internal desire others. Pressure groups and lobbies and powerful personalities are engines of change. Just think of a single individual, John A. Costello, and his declaration of a republic in 1949 or DeValera (Dr McQuaid perhaps in the shadows) and his constitution of 1937.

Irish society is changing again. Some think it is being remade or re-invented in a highly artificial way this time by a tiny minority. People suspect that the culprits are self-appointed gurus, the so-called liberals maybe, who have an exclusivist agenda and who operate in a covert and manipulative manner that is undemocratic and disdainful of ordinary citizens. That's a mouthful. It may also be accurate.

People's suspicion goes further. The kind of society that is being imposed on us by a few is foreign to our culture, history, religion, tradition and historical identity. The end result will be an ideological or a moral blight to parallel the social blight of the Famine or the blight of bungalows (I live in one) and middle class housing estates with gentrified English names that is said to sicken the Irish townland and the traditional Irish architectural landscape.

If the self-appointed gurus are to succeed in fashioning their new Irish society for themselves and for us plebs, whom they see as the unenlightened and 'the great unwashed' of the present age, they must first purge the old society we are stuck in. You and I, of course, are supposed to sit on the fence and either pretend not to notice or, if we do, to applaud the makeover. Is it possible that they do not see how keenly they re-incarnate the imperial arrogance of the colonial age? Maybe they do but think it's well worth it. Besides, haven't we lived long enough under the blighted fascism of the church and insular Irishism, and wouldn't any advance from that be liberation indeed?

A strategy is needed to achieve the new makeover. What is it? The strategy is to negate the Catholic-nationalist axis that still largely survives, if not by eliminating it at least by neutralising it. This Catholic-nationalist axis is, I suspect, mainly a state of mind. But it is said to infect those who still go the Mass (a great number by international standards) and has been for long the all-pervading Irish reality even if it is now in process of becoming a nostalgia. It still has wellsprings of influence with a majority of the Irish people and there is always the unhappy chance (for the makeover gurus) that its political and moral clout could be fired up again.

The Catholic-nationalist axis is the alignment of the triumphant church with the narrow social vision and values of past governments. The bishops may have lost much of their voice and our government may no longer feel the need of the church as a partner because of our economic success and our European immersion, yet the alliance of church and state is largely still there to be utilised if any bubbles should burst. One never knows! Hence the Catholic-nationalist axis is still a perceived threat to those who would re-invent Ireland to their own hearts' desire.

The gurus of change must be pleased that so much of their work is being done for them by the church itself. It is being done by the public's disenchantment with church-state relations in past generations. It is being done by the recent scandals and confusion. It is being done by the absence of intelligent adult religious education and preaching. It is being done by the failure of bishops' pastorals to reach the person in the pew. It is being done by the general absence of the bishops from the national dialogue. We seldom see them or their spokespersons in other than crisis appearances to answer the latest poll on declining church attendances and declining vocations.

It is being done by Catholic papers, official and unofficial, that are available at the parish church doors. I find that they tend to be confrontational and condemnatory and too quick on the trigger. They could be a great tool of adult religious education and formation, presenting an analysis of *both* sides of any social or religious issue and explaining the church's position as persuasively as possible. It is being done by lay people with their moving statues, apocalyptic warnings, myriad Marian appearances, and miracles forever on their minds. Would they all rest awhile in the Lord! It is being done by politicians and bankers and investors and developers and journalists, usually from our 'best' religious schools, who were never taught ethics apparently and who wouldn't recognise an ethic even if it were the first thing they saw on their laptop each morning. They would merely nod and wink at it. They have done immense social and religious damage to the young especially. It is being done by the failure of the authorities and the theologians in the church, despite the nice words, to live the relationship and respect the rights of each other's office, charism and contribution. It is being done by the perceived reduction of the gospel, grace and salvation to the all-consuming priority of the life issues. A generation or two ago we had the reduction of the gospel to the all-consuming priority of sex. There are many gospels in the gospel of Jesus. The gospel of pro-life is only one of them.

The goal of the gurus is to bring into being a modern, cosmopolitan, European, secular-humanist Ireland. The new sensitivity to what is called political correctness may be a sign of it – for example, religion should be an entirely private matter. I don't have an axe to grind with most of the agenda of political correctitude. I, too, disagree with the church poking its nose into everything. I agree with personal freedom, with personal responsibility, with equality of human and civil rights for the non-religious and the religious, the believer and the agnostic, the woman and the man, the heterosexual and the homosexual, the child and the adult. I agree with civility, decency, humanity and modernity. I believe in the values of education and consensus, in the open forum and the open marketplace, in truly humanistic development and the death of all sacred cows.

I agree with the gurus in disagreeing with xenophobia and homophobia, insularism, parochialism, narrow nationalism, church triumphalism and that smallness of intellect and heart that is typified in the national traits of jealousy, bemoaning, belittlement and begrudgery.

But I disagree with the gurus too. Unlike them, I do not have a particularly Romantic view of Europe. On the contrary, I believe that Europe is a political fracture and that it remains an ethnic and military faultline. Europe is weighted precariously by its history. Instead of a Romantic view of Europe I have a hopeful view of Europe. I admire those who wish to fashion a new Europe from such delicate roots. I agree with their effort to moderate all its explosive nationalisms but I find little comfort in their rather pagan values as a substitute for the best of our own traditional ones. In the area of personal and social ethics the new is not so far showing itself to be better than the old, if only because European ethics has been gutted of God.

I disagree with the gurus too in that I do not have a particularly Romantic view of humanity. I have a Christian view of humanity. Humans are flawed for all their greatness. That means that the gurus are flawed too. And the gurus, as the newest revolutionaries and visionaries in the land, are in the pattern of the old ones they despise. They too are a select group, they are another Sinn Féin (as in 'ourselves alone') and they are elitist; they are cocksure, they have an agenda, they see the future, and they will implement their vision of how things should be. And they will do it for the rest of us whether we like it or not. They have long since answered the question about how they know what kind of society the Irish people want and what the New Ireland is to be. All they have to do, they say, is look into their own hearts. Didn't we hear that one before?

Unlike the gurus, I do not accept the premise that the new Ireland can detach easily from the historical and cultural antecedents that the gurus say have stunted it thus far and that prevent it from embracing modernity and humanism. I may, of course, be wrong. I may be a part of the offending 'historical and cultural antecedents' myself and be too old and too blind to see. After all, we now have a majority of people in the nation for whom, unlike for me, pre-Vatican II and the ballroom of romance are ancient history. And we have seen stone-age societies and nineteenth century economies jump past all sorts of cultural traditions and embrace the late twentieth century with apparent ease. On the other hand, we have seen the Nigerias and Yugoslavias of the world regress. And how!

At any rate, I disagree with the gurus in the matter of the new conformity that I and others are being straddled with in order to fulfil their new vision. It smacks of elitist imposition and it is a repetition of the pressure and conformity that pockmark Irish history and that should gall at least as deeply as the old colonialist conformity and the old Catholic-nationalist conformity. Are we exchanging one conformity for another? If we are, then the new society is already as unliberated and as uncivil as the old. Do we ever learn anything from history?

Whatever shape the new Ireland finally settles into should not be the shape of any set of gurus. It should be the shape allowed by this, our first fully educated and emancipated generation. The young generation have the numbers, the money and the vote. It's up to them. They do not have to follow the models that Celtic romanticism, narrow nationalism, triumphalistic Catholicism and Dev's heart wished to impose. But neither do they have to accept the remake model of any elitist group. They can, of course, if they wish and if they're too self-preoccupied to develop their own as something that is still markedly Irish rather than an off-the-shelf European clone. It's another terrible beauty being born and it has become their personal responsibility.

Whatever the shape of their future, I urge them not to allow the New Ireland to sanitise too much of the past. I urge them not to sanitise the church out of the equation altogether. Social history has too many models and makeovers on the scrapheap. And I remind them of Will Durant's advisory on the value of an institution such as the church: 'There is no significant example in history, before our time, of a society successfully maintaining moral life without the aid of religion.'[15] It is this, more than a bursting economic bubble, that could bring the New Ireland down, no matter what shape it assumes. Just look at the moral rubble of the off-shore accounts and the bogus accounts and the tribunals. If they represent what we did with the help of religion, what might we do without it?

How can they? They signed up to the rules

Pat Kenny was interviewing a priest on *The Late, Late Show.* The priest had left the ministry and planned to marry. He wanted to remain a priest but could not as the church does not allow married priests. Asked why he saw no contradiction in breaking his vow of celibacy while married people are expected to keep theirs, he said that marriage is a sacrament but celibacy is a man-made rule. 'But you signed up to the rules,' said Kenny. The audience was divided. There were those who held for rules and those who held for freedom and love.

There's no doubt that people are divided on the issue of priests leaving to get married. For some it's a step in the right direction. It's an issue of personal freedom over institutional control. For others it's a disappointment and a bad example for all the people out there who are struggling to live up to their marriage vows and various responsibilities.

'How can the church be serious about the shortage of vocations when it lets men go over a thing like celibacy?' a young woman asked. 'How can you turn your back on the people?' countered a middle-aged man. It was clear that age and generation have a lot to do with the way people react.

I have the feeling that most people, whatever their relationship with the church, don't like to see priests leaving. It's rather like the feeling we have when too many politicians and professional leaders at the top let us down and our familiar and dependable world starts showing large cracks. Somehow we're all threatened. We can tolerate the occasional rainy day but not what appears to be a never-ending deluge. It's bad for morale.

Even young people, who seem so self-sufficient in their own world with their own agenda, take notice. It is as though their sixth sense tells them that discontent in the leadership levels of society may well affect them in some way later on and that their free-flowing lifestyle will be impacted. And it will. Already, the lack of nuns, priests, and brothers and the drying-up of vocations is causing the church to hand over educational, medical and various institutions of care to the state and to private groups. This, of course, can have positive as well as negative effects. But of one thing we can be sure: the young people will have to dig deeper into their pockets for themselves and their children in the coming years because of the shortage of vocations. Priests, nuns and brothers have been cheap labour for governments in many countries. That is one consequence of the decline in vocations that is documented in the US and Canada and that is visible in the international community.

Let's get back to Pat Kenny and his comment: 'But you signed up to the rules.' There are rules and there are rules! The priest on the TV show did sign up for celibacy. But he said that celibacy is only a man-made rule; that it is not the same as the marriage vow. Therefore he didn't see any big deal in breaking that rule. My take on his comment is as follows.

Celibacy (the rule to stay unmarried) is not exactly a man-made rule. It is an evangelical counsel. That means, it is something encouraged by Jesus in the gospel. (See Mt 19:12) It is not for everyone. But, as a counsel from Christ, it should be practised in the church by some people. If it is not, the church is not fulfilling all the requirements laid down by Jesus for his church. However, Jesus says in the same verse, 'Let him accept it who can.' That raises the issue of personal choice as opposed to institutional imposition. The church makes celibacy a mandatory requirement for every man who believes he is called to priesthood. He has no choice. He has to 'buy it as part of the package' for priesthood.

Now there are already people in the church, other than diocesan priests, who practise the charism of celibacy. They are called the Religious. They are nuns and brothers and religious order priests. They live what's called the common or community life. You cannot imagine their kind of life without celibacy. Celibacy fits them perfectly. However, the priest on TV was a diocesan priest. Diocesan priests do not live the common or community life. Celibacy is not core or crucial to their calling. Nevertheless, the church has decided that they too must live the celibate life. In that sense, you can say the priest on TV was right when he called his celibacy a man-made rule that is not necessary for priesthood. Celibacy is not necessary for priesthood. St Peter, for instance, was a married man. So why does the church impose it on diocesan priests when it's already practised by the religious orders, and the church is thereby already fulfilling the Lord's counsel?

But the priest was wrong if he gave the impression, which I feel he did, that celibacy is man-made in the sense that some Pope in history or some church committee dreamed it up and that Jesus never said anything about it.

I agree with the priest in this: signing up to the rule of celibacy is not the same as signing up to your marriage vows. The vow to permanently and exclusively love one person is of the essence of marriage. This rule cannot be broken without breaking the marriage itself. The TV priest's celibacy is not essential to his priesthood nor to his exercise of the priesthood. That's why there's a huge difference between 'signing up to the rules' when it involves celibacy and 'signing up to the rules' when it involves marriage. There are rules and there are rules! They are not all the same.

What arguments can be raised in favour of celibacy for *all* priests and what points can be made in opposition?

The arguments in favour of celibacy for all priests fall into two categories. Broadly, these are either practical or theological. Practically, there are some observations made by St Paul that influence the church's rule of celibacy. One is in 1 Cor 7:27: 'Are you free from a wife? Do not seek a wife.' The church finds that advice apt for all priests. Paul, however, is speaking to men and women, not specifically to priests. He speaks, as the scholars tell us, with the expectation of the second coming of Christ in mind. It will happen at any moment. So he urges everyone to keep to their present condition and not to change their status lest they be distracted and therefore unprepared for the Lord's arrival. In this context, the line is not an argument for or against marriage as such or for or against celibacy for priests.

A few lines later Paul writes: 'I want you to be free from anxieties ... the married man is anxious about the affairs of the world, how to please his wife.' (1 Cor 7:32-33) Here again, Paul is writing to Christian men and women and not specifically to priests. However, the church takes this line, considers it appropriate for priests, and uses it as an argument in favour of priestly celibacy. It has a point – but it is a practical point and not a theological one. A married parish priest would have to please his wife and divide his time between family and the parishioners. To use current coin: How much quality time could a busy parish priest give to his marriage, his wife and his children? Is it not true that his life, especially in a modern urban setting, is one of constant interruptions and constant demands from others? If marriage and family life are more stressed and vulnerable today than ever before, why should the people's priests get caught in them? And in addition, if priests marry we should expect their divorce rate to be equivalent to the general rate. Who wants to see their priests get into the mess and the stress that modern divorce is?

These are practical considerations and the church should not be brushed aside for raising them. However, the church can be challenged over giving them a prominence they simply do not deserve. For instance, the non-Catholic churches have married clergy and marriage does not appear to be an unusual burden for them. In fact, there are hundreds of married priests even in the Roman Catholic Church. They are converts from other denominations. Some of these family men are fulltime Catholic parish priests and curates. They seem to be doing just fine.

Favouring, though not promoting, a married diocesan clergy is this third observation from St Paul. Paul is addressing Timothy, the man he ordained a bishop. 'A bishop must be above reproach, married only once.' (1 Tim 3:2) Paul is saying that a bishop should be of unquestionable character and married only to one woman. There's no celibacy here!

Another practical matter in the discussion on married priests is the financial one. How would the church (i.e. the people) support them, their wives and their families? Certainly there would have to be major adjustments in church finances. Could a country parish support married priests? A few years ago priests themselves said no. With the new Irish economy? – maybe.

If priests married, the church in a country like the US, where there is no state support for Catholic schools, would have to face the option of either closing all its parochial schools or operating just a few for the elite that could afford them. That would raise the spectre of a financial *and* a racial divide in dioceses and parishes. The parish monies that presently subsidise US Catholic education and keep the schools open to all would have to go instead to sustain a married clergy.

For most priests of my acquaintance a critical issue is that celibacy prioritises institutional control over personal freedom. It is often phrased this way by priests themselves: If priests married, Rome would lose most of its control over them. But that can be used as an argument for and against celibacy equally. Everyone likes freedom. It should be promoted. On the other hand, society and its institutions are, by their very nature, controlling agents, and people understand that. People more or less want it that way.

The Late, Late Show did not deal with the heart of the matter. Here we move into theology as such. The heart of the matter is an old view of celibate priesthood that is raised again by Vatican II and treated later at length by John Paul II. In the *Decree on the Life and Ministry of Priests* (#2), the council states: '[Through ordination] priests are signed with a special character and so are configured to Christ … in such a way that they are able to act in the person of Christ the head.'

The priest has a special identity with Christ. It is conferred by the 'character' of his ordination. He is 'configured' to Christ in a way the layperson is not. He acts in the person of Christ in a way the layperson cannot. We might think that all that's being talked about here is the obvious fact that the priest does things Christ did that the layperson cannot do – absolve sins and change bread and wine into the Body and Blood of the Lord. But John Paul II has a different and a deeper understanding of what the council meant. In addressing a group of American bishops (9/9/83), he returns to the council's words 'configured to Christ'. He says that celibacy reflects that configuring and fills it out. What does he mean?

In his writings the Pope sees the priest 'as Christ' in his whole lifestyle and not only when standing *in persona Christi* as he celebrates Mass and hears confessions. The priest is in the person of Christ in a way that includes Christ's celibacy and his male sexuality (referred to in *Novo incipiente nostro* [1979] and *Pastores dabo vobis*

[1992]). This is a controversial gloss or spin on the council's theology of priesthood. It means that all the practical arguments we outlined above and that call celibacy into question have no weight with the Pope. According to the Pope's theology, priests must remain celibate in order to *properly* express what it means for one to be 'in the person of Christ' the priest.

John Paul II's theology is controversial. He has moved a view of celibacy as fitting for priesthood up to the level of almost theological requirement. His theology affects more than the male priests who debate their celibacy. It affects our own married priests, at least psychologically, as well as the married clergy of the Orthodox Christian churches with whom we crave unity. It is also controversial with women, with those who advocate women's ordination, and with the Anglican Communion which has female bishops and priests, for the Pope insists that being 'in the person of Christ' as priest includes Jesus' male sexuality. The Pope's theology appears to abort the debate on celibacy and to end any hope for the ordination of women.

What, then, are we to make of St Peter? He was a Pope. And he was a married man. What are we to do with St Paul's advice to Timothy about the bishop being a man with only one wife? What are we to say about the hundreds of married men who serve today as parish priests and curates in our church with Rome's blessing?

The church would answer, I imagine, that these are the exceptions to the rule, and that there will always be exceptions, as in the case of married clergymen converting to Catholicism. The church will say that nonetheless celibacy remains the desired way of life for all priests and that it better configures them to Christ. The church will say that celibacy was always the desire of the church no matter how many generations it took for it to finally take hold – more or less – and become the norm for Catholic priests.

The synodal letter, *Ultimis temporibus* (1967), adds an element of eschatological theology in attempting to derail the debate on celibacy. It considers celibacy in light of the next life. It favours retaining celibacy because celibacy is a sign to modern men and women that this life is a passing thing. It favours celibacy for priests as a way of calling people back to 'the sublimity of faithful love and reveal[ing] the ultimate meaning of life.'(#4) In other words, the priest by his celibacy is a reminder to men and women that they should be faithful in their married life, that married love is earthbound, and that celibacy will be *everyone's* condition in heaven.

The official documentation we have looked at here, and it is only a sample, suggests to me that the church will hold firm to its tradition of celibacy against all odds. It does not matter, it seems, whether or not celibacy has done more harm than good for the church in the present or in the past; whether or not it sets up the church for more scandals and departures generation after generation into the misty future; whether or not we have more priestless Sunday liturgies around the world or more priestless rural parishes in Ireland; and whether or not fewer, overburdened priests carry a load that eventually crushes them and is an inspiration to no one. The church will hold out on this celibacy issue no matter the cost. Why?

For one thing, the present Pope has bound the church to celibacy more than any other Pope since the Reformation and he has underpinned it with his controversial theology of celibacy. For another, maybe the church believes an upsurge of celibate vocations is around the corner. Or maybe the church is willing to live with the losses and ignore the statistics that ask, in effect, if celibacy is a sign of anything worthwhile anymore or just a troublesome contradiction. Or maybe the church is happy to live with a poorer quality of vocations and fewer priests. Or maybe the church is full of a faith in God's providence that its critics cannot even comprehend. Or maybe the church is not listening to God in the signs of the times even as it thinks it is all ears to the Spirit. Is the official church being amazingly faithful or intrepidly stubborn? In the final analysis, I personally do not know. Only the Spirit does.

Does the following fact speak for the priest on the *Late, Late* or against him? Does it speak for celibacy or against it? More critically, does it speak for the pastoral wisdom of the church or for its pastoral blindness? Does it show what happens when a minor theology deflects the church from its central doctrine and mission? Let you be the judge. Here is the fact:

There are Catholic communities in Latin America that, in their entire 500 years of Catholicism, have never had a resident parish priest or curate. In other words, they have never been able to become what theology calls full ecclesial communities. They have never been fully church. Why did that happen, and why will it continue to happen?

Latino priests say that it's mainly because of Rome's stubbornness with regard to the rule of celibacy. I think that this sad vignette speaks volumes about the mind of Rome on the celibacy question for today and for tomorrow and for all our TV shows.

Lay consultation is a joke

In the immediate afterglow of Vatican II there was a widespread feeling that lay people would finally make it in the church. They would no longer be the inert group that had to put up with the infallibility of parish priests, that listened to boring sermons, and that had no say in the running of the church. Their function was to keep their mouths shut and pay all the bills. All that would change.

People felt that they had the numbers and that they, not so much the clergy, would determine parish priorities from then on. I remember enthusiastic discussions on how the people would select their priests and what demands they would make of the bishop. Even when more realistic minds tempered the enthusiasm and spoke in favour of priests retaining a major say, no lay person doubted that sweeping changes were on the way. The people and the clergy would be co-responsible for the pastoral life of the parish. We would never be church in the same old clericalist way again.

But a few people who knew a little church history did not get caught up in the unbridled enthusiasm. They knew that things would not be very different. The church had opposed lay control and lay 'interference' before. There were examples from the 1800s – such things as lay wardenships in Europe and lay trustees in America and American congregations 'buying' and 'importing' their own priest from the old countries like Prussia and Poland and Italy when they felt excluded by ethnic parishes, mainly Irish I'm sorry to say.

Church history signalled that the official church would never let real power – sacramental, pastoral, financial and administrative – slip from central clerical control.

The true role of the laity would remain as it had always been. It would have to develop along the traditional spiritual and lay apostolate lines. In fact, anyone reading the sixteen documents of the council would already have seen that there would be no substantive change for the lay person, and that there would be an even stronger centralisation of power in the Pope, in the bishops collectively, and in the local bishop. They would also have seen in the documents a theology of the laity that was spiritual, apostolic and located dominantly in the marketplace and not in the church. But then, how many people actually read the documents of the council?

But for a while the new enthusiasm caught everyone. It seemed to have substance when the consultative process was set up throughout the universal church. The very idea of consulting the laity was energising to many people. A new departure for the church! A bow to an educated generation, to democracy and to the signs of the times! There would be a diocesan-wide council of the laity. In large dioceses there would be regional councils as well. There would be a parish council and there would be parish committees involving the laity in everything from liturgy to finance. Parishes would be consulted when a new parish priest was appointed. The new appointee would match the profile of the parish and the needs expressed by the parishioners.

The bishop, too, would be moderated by a council of priests, a council of religious, and a council of laity. It looked like the church was bending over backwards to accommodate the laity and their aspirations.

Well, here we are a third of a century after the council and what have we? We have large sections of the church where most of the above lay involvement does not exist in any meaningful way. We have other large sections where it has been tried but the initial enthusiasm has been so tempered by the realities that the lay consultative process is like a car stuck in neutral. We have some dioceses and parishes with a high degree of lay participation, lay planning and lay co-responsibility with the clergy. But even these are experiencing difficulties. The whole question of lay consultation or lay involvement or lay co-responsibility rests on what I call – for want of a better phrase – a theology of limitations. What does that mean?

I mean that Vatican II has no theology of the laity that fits what we have been describing or that matches the enthusiasm that people assumed was in the books. Church law, which interprets theology in practice, has a very restrictive understanding of such things as lay participation, lay involvement in parish and diocesan life, and lay co-responsibility for church life. The laity are not really determinative of things in the church. Their role is 'only consultative.' That's the nub of the matter.

'Consultative' simply means they can be listened to or ignored or overruled. By whom? By the clergy. And the clergy can be overruled by the bishop, and the bishop by the Pope. Are we back where we started? Probably. The restrictive understanding of the laity's role is found not only in the traditional understanding of the laity's position in the church; it is found in the new Code of church law. And now again it has been re-affirmed in the Roman instruction, *Questions Regarding the Collaboration of the Non-Ordained Faithful*, issued in November 1997. Even though this document deals primarily with ministry, it says clearly that parish councils and parish committees *are only consultative.*

Lay consultation is a joke then for people who thought that Vatican II was going to make them determining agents in their church. It is a joke for those who believed democracy was about to fall on their parish. It is a joke for those who do not know the church's prior theology and history or who have forgotten the hierarchical nature of the church and of authority and decision-making within it. It is a joke for those people of great expertise and limited time who find that their consultation can be brushed aside by a clerical dictum, sometimes a whim, or by the theology and church law they are not aware of. They do not realise how deeply the hierarchical order goes to the heart of how the official church understands itself.

Lay consultation, understood as a joke, raises once again the need of adult religious education, if only so that people and priests read from the same page, can speak to each other out of a common theology, and appreciate the mindset each brings to bear on parish life and all its aspects.

On the other hand, lay consultation does not have to be a joke. Despite all we've just said it can be pursued on many levels. It can even be determinative and not just consultative on many levels and on issues affecting the parish: education, liturgy, apostolate, spiritual programmes, even finances. So much depends on the mutual confidence of priest and people in each other. The only caveats need be the restraints imposed *a priori* by theology and law. One might argue that those restraints are too many and too fundamental to allow of any worthwhile consultation and determination. They are to some people, but not to others. A great deal can be accomplished within the restraints. Speaking from my own experience I can say that most of the day-to-day life of the parish is untouched by the limits we have mentioned above. There is, therefore, huge scope for co-responsibility and determinative collaboration by a parish's people and its priests.

It may have been a bit dishonest to the laity from the very beginning for the church to talk about its new vision of itself as the people of God, of the laity's co-responsibility for preaching the gospel, and of their vocation to participate actively and enthusiastically in church and parish life. It masked the real limits that it had in mind for the people despite the language of shared responsibility. The church may counter and say that nothing was dishonest, that all was clear as crystal in the official documents. And indeed it was – to the trained eye. That assumes that everyone read the documents and understood them readily. They didn't. And they couldn't. Looking back on that afterglow that followed the council I don't remember the church's leadership doing much of anything to moderate the lay enthusiasm and re-educate their expectations. It would have saved us all a lot frustration and heartache.

A woman's place is not in the church

People are surprised when they hear that the vast majority of Catholic women around the world are quite happy with their place in the church. We are not talking only about women in the second and third worlds. We're also talking about women in the first world, the so-called developed world to which we belong.

You may suspect, however, that many of these are à la carte Catholic women and that they are able to stay in the church and be relatively happy there only because they reject some of the church's teaching. That may be true. On the other hand, I don't believe there is such a person as a 100% Catholic. I've met many, of course, who think they are.

It's impossible to define what a 100% Catholic is. I suppose the definition of such a person would have to include the perfection of religious knowledge and of spiritual living in Christ. Not even the canonised saints come up to this standard, never mind the Pope and the bishop and the parish priest.

Then there's that whole issue in educational psychology of human perception, comprehension and realisation. These are big words for the way we understand and practise our faith, for the way we only partially understand and partially practise the faith. Or any faith. Or anything.

Most people – women as well as men – try to do their best within the organisations to which they belong and that includes their church affiliation. Fullness exists only on paper and in heaven.

My point is that the vast majority of Catholic women reject the widespread assumption that women cannot find a place or personal fulfilment in the church. They can and they do, apparently. However, a significant minority of Catholic women are very upset with the church because they cannot find their place or personal fulfilment in it. They find that they are not the women the church assumes all women should be and they see their concerns as ones that the church is not interested in and will never address. They are probably right. In saying that, I am not taking a stand with the church against them. I'm stating what I suspect is simply a fact and a troublesome one at that.

I say troublesome because we always gloried in the belief that gospel and grace and church were open to all and fulfilling to all. The church is 'the universal sacrament of salvation,' says Vatican II, and all should 'find their home in her.' (See *Lumen Gentium*, #1) Is the church now imposing restrictions on who belongs, or are some women falsely re-defining womanhood and the church?

Many women of child-bearing age feel they are treated as second-class citizens in the church over the matter of birth control. Others feel the same way because they are denied ordination. There are other perceived injustices. Spiritual, legal and administrative power is lodged in the male clerical caste. The equality and respect that should normally come to women of faith is denied them by this male exclusivism. Theology has been largely a male enterprise and its thought categories and presentation show this. Gender and language inclusiveness in the liturgy is blocked or allowed only a trickle-down tokenism in response to constant protest and pressure. The priestly mentality, whether among the old or the young, remains suspicious of women. And the democratic drive for women's equality in rights and opportunities that should find its champion in Jesus' church finds instead one of its chief obstacles.

Some women (and men too) have dropped out of the institutional church altogether because they see the deeper issue that lies beneath all these questions of equal rights, women's control over their bodies, and women's ordination. On a deeper level these people see the Catholic Church's limitations on women as a contradiction of humanism, even of Christian humanism. For them, Christian humanism is better found in other Christian churches. All our church's talk about the major place it gives to Mary in the church, and the influence it has allowed female saints and female mystics and foundresses to exercise in the church, is only shadow boxing and a dancing around the perimeter. It does not get to the core issue. The core issue is the equality of women in the church expressed in structures and roles of authority and of ordination that clearly prove it.

The church has made some responses. It has produced a fine theology of woman through the pen of John Paul II (*The Dignity of Woman,* 1988). I don't know of a comparable theology of man. The church has said it does not believe it has the 'competency' to ordain women. That means that the church doesn't believe it has the authority from Christ, the gospel or sacred tradition to ordain them, and that to attempt to do so would be an empty fabrication. However, it has never said it would like to ordain them if it could. I find that missing courtesy a significant statement in itself. In the same manner, the church has said that artificial means of birth control are opposed to God's will as it is expressed in natural law. Again, the church feels it cannot satisfy this demand because it does not have the 'competency' to revoke God's will which it says is expressed in natural law. But, then, there are several opinions on what natural law is and they are not all the church's version.

The church has responded to women's concerns by appointing women to various offices in the church that were traditionally the domain of men, e.g. as chancellors of dioceses and members of boards of management and of consultation. However, there may be no real gain for women nor inroad here into the male domain since other new clerical offices have also appeared at the same time. An example. Some years ago, if you were the chancellor of a diocese you were the major player in the day-to-day life of a diocese. Perhaps the chancellor's greatest power lay in his ability to make the diocesan clergy changes, which the bishop then rubber-stamped. We have female chancellors today but they do not have that power. It has gone to a new office, the vicar for the clergy, who is, of course, a male priest.

So, we see that the church has responded to some women's concerns but we also see little change in the dominant male status quo. The birth control and ordination issues seem to have been frozen by the (male) church authorities. But the real issue in all of this, an issue perhaps more fundamental than women's rights, is the question: Does the church remain the great promoter of humanism that it has historically claimed to be or is it now a major obstacle? Has time caught up with the church, and has the modern democracy of full human and civil rights exposed the church's limitations? Are these limitations of the essence of the church in the sense that they cannot be changed? And does that leave the church of the coming years an institution in which some women will feel less and less at home? And will it justify these women when they tell their friends that a woman's place is not in the Catholic Church?

An addiction to stones and bones

'How do you feel about the present church?' I asked a friend. I thought he would say, predictably, that things were bad at the moment but that they would get better. 'The church here is like the island of Ireland in relation to the continent,' he said. 'It's out by the side of things.'

I pressed him a bit. He said: 'There is no real theology here. I don't think there has been for hundreds of years. All we've had is politicised religion in the North and flag waving for Rome in the South. Throw in dead ritual. No roots at all there for spirituality to grow out of. No wonder people abandon it in droves. They see through it. It's empty.' Was he not being too negative, I suggested. He said he wasn't. I said that some hopeful efforts were being made to put life into the church. 'Like what?' he asked. I said: 'What about the new interest in Celtic spirituality? What about the bishops' proposal that the faith might be re-awakened by returning to our roots through visits to holy wells and old cemeteries and traditional pilgrimage sites?' He dismissed that. 'An addiction to stones and bones,' he said.

He said a lot more. However, those words – an addiction to stones and bones – have stayed with me. Like all pithy phrases it is at best a half-truth. It does, however, say more about what is missing from our faith than what is present to it. And maybe it also suggests that we are searching in the wrong places for the wellspring of a 21st-century faith.

I find that for myself old places – the stones and bones – are important. When you are an emigrant and far from home places back in Ireland and the people who inhabited them are a constant memory and, I feel, a grace. I went back to the States after each summer holiday and found that my Irish photos never changed. They were pictures of the parents and the siblings and their children. All that happened from year to year was that the parents and the siblings grew greyer and the children gradually grew up.

There were pictures of classmates too. They were home for a holiday like myself. The photos showed that we bumped into one another in the places familiar to our childhood. The places were always the narrow town streets that were laid out by the Normans and on which 800 years of our generations had played. The places were also King John's castle, the Ramparts, the new cemetery on the fairy fort, the old cemetery by the Dominican priory, and the pre-Reformation cemetery in the grounds of the Church of Ireland. These were our places of play and discovery and growing up more than of prayer and holiness; we, the quick, tumbling and laughing with ease above the generations of our dead. We had no sense of doing anything irreverent in those holy places. The dead were *our* dead and we felt quite at home puffing a Woodbine or mowing down Red Indians above them.

My parents are among the dead now, and my own place is ready for me beside them. I will have no problem with children playing above my head even if the correctness of the new social order prevents them from dragging on a Woodbine and mowing down an ethnic group.

We graduated eventually, of course, from such things to an interest in the history of those places and an interest in the men and women who built them and who finally were buried in them. They were the de Burgo's and the de Bermingham's; the Dominicans and the mendicants; the emissaries carrying the charter from Rome that established the Dominican university against whose ruined wall we learned to play handball. They were the commoners under the flagstones at our feet whose names were indecipherable but whose trade was clear enough: the sign of the carpenter, the sign of the sheep shearer, the sign of the smith.

Prior generations had left gaps in the river embankment for cattle to be watered and clothes to be washed at the river's level (They're closed up now). This showed us that the town once sloped down to the river and we could tell how high the embankments were raised by the later generations. Eight hundred years of us had put our feet in the river at the exact same spot. How many men and women, knights and soldiers and monks, boys and girls had stood there down the ages and asked their questions of the river? I was always conscious, standing there in Abbey Row, of the flow of faith that knit all those people together and that knit me to them. I was just a speck in the continuum of life and faith that faded into the past and equally faded into the future.

My town – stones and bones – was always a spiritual experience for me. Out foreign, as we used to say, I remembered it equally in times of tranquillity and agitation. It calmed me and it held me close. My town, Athenry, is a sacred place to me. And all of that is why I believe in the value of 'stones and bones.' I know that graces emerge from them.

But, as I said earlier, perhaps 'an addiction to stones and bones' also points to what is missing from our faith, and to what must be present if faith is to find wide acceptance in the 21st century. Where is the wellspring that is missing? Surely, it is the word of God. 'The words I spoke to you are spirit ... and they are life.' (Jn 6:63, 68) The word of God speaks directly to the human heart in a way that neither ritual nor stone nor anything else can. That is its attraction, and God obviously intended it that way.

Our church has not been a great promoter of the word of God from Gutenberg to Vatican II. The reasons given for this vary but they all seem to have the word 'danger' attached to them. There was danger in putting 'the Book' into people's hands. (There's always danger for authority in books!). There was the danger inherent in private interpretation of God's word. There was the danger that people would put the bible ahead of the church. There was danger from the autonomy and personalisation that are inherent in the word of God with their tendency to undermine church authority. And the danger of competing interpretations and consequent confusion and factionalism. There was danger from the politicisation of the word of God – from the bible co-opted by Protestants, seen as the badge of Protestantism, a fulcrum of independence, and a tool for anti-Catholicism. In these circumstances, the word of God, as the primary educator of God's people, declined in our church. It declined elsewhere too as one may judge from its abuse as a tool of empire-building for kings and Kaisers and as heartless jingoism in the North.

Vatican II attempted to set things right with the word of God. The scripture is certainly more prominent in the liturgy today as it is in our renewed theology and seminary courses. Private and prayerful reading of the bible is encouraged. Personal formation through the word of God is encouraged. But the old caveats remain. Scripture must be read within the living tradition of the church. That caveat subjects bible interpretation to church authority. And scripture is not above the church because the Christian faith, we are told, is not a religion of the book. That caveat ensures the central importance of the church.

Nonetheless, Vatican II makes it clear enough that the word of God is crucial to proper Christian formation. In this sense, our addiction to stones and bones, to novenas and relics, to statues and pilgrimages does not have to end but it should now play second fiddle to God's word and be judged and purified by that word.

Many contemporary Catholics who are dedicated to the word of God are disappointed over our Jubilee celebrations. They see once again an official emphasis on the old 'stones and bones' spirituality. They see a growing trend towards dim spiritualities based on popular psychology and nature. But they see very little emphasis on scriptural understanding and appreciation and real Christian formation through God's word. Certainly, there is no push anywhere in our church for a comprehensive engagement with that word.

Some Catholics do not believe that there is enough in the extra-biblical sources, popular though they be, to encounter the living God in our new time and circumstances and challenges. Nor is it enough for them, they say, to hear a few scriptures proclaimed well or poorly at Sunday Mass. The past thirty-five years since the council appear to prove that. They feel that the council itself may well have desired a comprehensive spiritual renewal based on word and sacrament but that it finally settled for the traditional stress on sacrament and ritual to the detriment of the word of God. At any rate, they have not been renewed in their relationship with Jesus by Vatican II and the liturgical turmoil it engendered. And they feel that there is not enough in the traditional devotions and in the 'stones and bones' spirituality to renew their faith in a literate age.

According to the scriptures, we are fashioned into God's holy people by his word. And that takes serious engagement and study.

Our roots have to be down deep in the word of God to really touch him and to develop spiritually. This is true for every Christian generation and we can not be the exception. Without the word of God at our feet and in our hearts it is surprisingly easy to avoid God even in the middle of the church. I have seen this in prelates and I have seen it in myself.

I suspect there are parallels in psychology and emotion, in experiences of insight and insult, in gains and losses, in private loneliness and hope between the present generation of spiritual searchers and the prophet Jeremiah. And because of these parallels I think they are the kind of searchers who, once immersed in the word of God, would come to echo the prophet: 'Your words were found, and I ate them, and your words became to me a joy and the delight of my heart.' (Jer 15:16)

Who's really responsible for Ansbacher?

The Ansbacher deposits came to light during the McCracken Tribunal in 1997. These monies were technically offshore accounts not subject to tax. However, the depositors had use of these monies as if they were ordinary accounts at their local bank. This crooked operation was but a part of a greater network of fraud.

Who was behind the Ansbacher scheme and who were the depositors? Names don't matter here. The real issue is Irish ethics. What matters is that most of them came from 'good' families and went to our 'best' schools. That raises the question of their education and what their many years of religious instruction consisted of. It is possible, of course, that some of them thought they were part of a legitimate tax-avoidance scheme. It is probable that most of them were too shrewd not to know the full story. What also matters is that their shenanigans have been replicated by thousands of others before and since – investors, bankers, politicians, and even the 'plain people of Ireland.' It has gone on for decades. Ansbacher is a word that may yet stand as a synonym for tax evasion Irish style.

Since Ansbacher we have become familiar with the umpteen thousands of bogus non-resident accounts. We have long been experts in the tax dodges that are as common to the whole world as to ourselves – the two sets of books, the money paid in cash under the table, and the 'in kind' unreported exchanges. Some see tax evasion as fun and games. Others see it as a challenge to their intellectual prowess in the way hackers love to break computer codes. But in the end, all of them defraud the taxman and, of course, they place the burden of paying the national bills and the national debt on the backs of the honest taxpayers. That is horribly unjust. It is especially unconscionable in critical financial times and Ireland has known many such times. Such a time was the Ansbacher decades.

Now I'm no great supporter of the Irish taxation bands. They are arguably too high for everyone and far too high for the average wage earner. But I do believe in the necessity of taxation for the common good and in everyone's obligation to pay their fair share.

The Ansbacher scandal and its many financial relatives do not show us, as a people, to any great advantage. When all of these financial scandals are joined to all the other scandalous stories of modern Ireland, we present a sad sight. These modern Irish stories depict us as materialistic, greedy, self-centred and predatory. It is the latest version of the sow eating her own farrow.

It underlines a sober reality. All the characters in these Irish stories, be they the big fish or the minnows, are sailing through the life of the nation and through their own personal lives untouched by the ethical standards of their religion. Their religion has no bearing on their social behaviour. How can that be? So many of them come from 'good' families and were educated at our 'best' schools. Questions must be asked. Indeed, that's all we seem to be doing these days in Ireland: questions about our lack of morals and about the church's role in this.

What kind of Christianity was taught them? Was there any mention of civic duty? Was love of country taught? Were the only models of patriotism those of Pearse and 1916, the GPO and the rifle, and wrapping the green flag 'round me, boys? Did anyone tell them that the contemporary form of patriotism is social responsibility?

Was their schooling all fun and games, the old school tie, kicking for touch, and the number of silver cups in the trophy cabinet? Was the only eye on them the one that saw them as future captains of industry and commerce and therefore potential for future donations to dear old *alma mater*? Is it again the old story of the institution becoming more important than the human enterprise that should be its *raison d'être,* the god that must be protected and prospered no matter the missing moral bits? It would seem so. Irish education for decades is a story of missing bits – patriotism in the true sense and social ethics among the bits.

Most of these cheaters, big and small, are in church every week. Apparently nothing is happening there either in ritual or in homily that convinces them of the integral connection between the faith they profess and its practice, between liturgy and life. What is my point? It is simply this. Religion has failed these people. At least, the kind of disconnected religion they received at school failed them. And it continues to fail them in their parish churches. It has failed them in the same way it has failed all the other casualties of religion that have come to public notice in our day and that we profess to be shocked over.

Religion, like God, is a trinity. It is the business of religion to give life meaning. It is the business of religion to connect people intimately with their God. And it is the business of religion to help people translate the stuff of everyday existence from a set of temptations into a set of opportunities and grace. Were the young cheaters shown how money, for example, is not an opportunity for stultifying greed but for personal and social enhancement? Someone may answer, Yes, we told them that. But telling is not enough. Education and religion are also about persuasion. They are about translation.

As one looks back at all the moral misdeeds that have come to light spanning many decades, one is aware of their common denominator. It is the failure in ethics education. The church is the self-professed moral teacher of us all. The church is the one that was entrusted with the education of generations of us. Ansbacher says it has failed in its job of translating the stuff of life through the word of God. The words of the young emigrant Gar O'Donnell to his parish priest in Brian Friel's drama *Philadelphia, Here I Come!* were written when most of the Ansbacher generation were still in their Catholic schools and a few not long gone from them. Gar's world was not that of the Celtic Tiger and big money and offshore accounts. His world was that of barren soil, having to leave home, and the emigrant ship. The issue is still translation. Listen to him: 'But I'm wasting my time with you, Canon – because you could translate all this loneliness, this groping, this dreadful bloody buffoonery into Christian terms that would make life bearable for all. And yet you don't say a word. Why, Canon? Why, arid Canon? Isn't this your job? – to translate?'[16]

Who, then, is really responsible for Ansbacher? Theology says the individual cheaters themselves. And that's true. They are responsible for their actions. And yet, Irish society sees the church hovering there in their background. The church is the one that claimed to have the authority to teach morality. It is the one that was in charge of the schools and of the ethical formation. And it is the one that was given the mandate of translating life in Christian terms by the Lord.

Human progress – technology or religion?

Are we humanised by technology or by religion? Do we become more human through technology or through religion? Does the human race progress on the basis of technology or of religion? There are two pat answers. One answer says that technology has worked wonders in advancing the quality of humanness through better health, education and welfare. It has released us from being beasts of burden. The other answer says that religion is fundamental to becoming authentically human.

People seldom leave well enough alone. Emotions and biases enter the debate. So both answers get tails added on. Religion is said to be a stumbling block to human progress. Technology is said to be a destroyer of culture and civilisation.

Older people tend to favour religion. Younger people tend to favour technology. Other people see the question as a false one. I think it is. The human race rides on the backs of both religion and technology, even if both have their limitations.

As to limitations, one can point to the times that religion has stood in the way of human progress. One thinks of Rome's opposition to modern democracy and to religious freedom. One thinks of the quasi-religious Luddite movement in England in the 1800s that smashed the early industrial machines. One thinks of the inbred suspicion that religion has towards novelty of any kind. One can also point to the instances in history where technology increased the range of war, the scale of destruction, the depth of human pain and left us with flattened cities and poisoned landscapes. With these histories, neither religion nor technology can claim to be a pure instrument of human progress.

Last year a friend of mine died. He was the dean of science fiction writers, A. E. van Vogt. I remember a discussion in his home on this subject. He was strong in praise of the blessings of technology. He contrasted his own life blessed by technology with his grandfather's hard life on a Canadian farm. You might have expected this praise anyway from the man who was writing of future technological worlds even before the Second World War.

He saw no hope for the world's burgeoning population without science and technology. Religion, he felt, had no responsibility to provide the food, shelter, health and education required by the planet's billions of people. Such massive provisioning was the responsibility of governments. It was a moral imperative for human ingenuity that could only be fulfilled through science and technology.

There were other sides to van Vogt you might not expect if you knew him only as a futuristic writer and a champion of science and technology. His books are published in many languages. His *Black Destroyer* is the inspiration for the movie classic *Alien*. One of his more philosophical sci-fi books was made into a movie in France. But none was made into a Hollywood movie because he would not let Hollywood write additional and gratuitous sex into any of them. He was of Dutch Calvinist background. That may explain his reverential attitude toward women and sex. And he went to Mass with his Catholic wife each Sunday and holyday. He had all the graces of what is called the old-fashioned Christian gentleman.

Yet he also wrote a book on 'the money personality' that is used by US corporations, and one on brainwashing techniques that was used by the military during the Korean War. He designed one of the most popular and effective language-learning programmes that has been in use in America for decades, and he devised mental health techniques in the early 1950s that parallel modern-day dianetics. Religion and technology were equally at home in this man.

But what did religion mean to him in terms of human progress? It's not easy to say. He had faith. He believed in God. He believed in the commandments. They were sensible guides to healthy living. They were also the word of God. He believed in moral goodness and moral badness and the need of accountability in this life and in the next. He practised the traditional Christian values. I do not know what his personal prayer life was because he never revealed that side of himself. He came from a Protestant tradition in which religion was a private matter between the believer and God. And, of course, he believed in heaven as God's future world beyond our technological world and beyond all of his own van Vogt future worlds. May he rest in peace.

In terms of the question before us in this chapter, I think van Vogt saw the answer this way. Religion's energy is directed to the afterlife. Therefore, its aim is not promoting human progress in this life. Religion is matter of personal faith. As such, it is two-dimensional. It is the private prayer life of the believer and it is the social ethic of loving your immediate neighbours. In this understanding, it is not the business of religion to engineer human progress and social development on the grand scale. Science and technology are responsible for those. However, science and technology should not be seen as secular things divorced from God. They are man's ingenuity for shaping a better world and that ingenuity is a gift from God.

van Vogt placed a moral responsibility on science and technology for human progress and the cultivation of the earth. If religion has a role in the earth's big social scene it is that of encouraging, rather politely, human and social progress.

As for myself, I see the role of religion in what I think is a fuller and more socially engaged light than did my friend. I see it much the way that European and American Protestant exponents of the so-called social gospel saw it in the late nineteenth and early twentieth centuries, and in the way the post-Vatican II church sees it today. In this theology, the total well-being (spiritual and temporal) of men and women is the goal of all economic and technological development. Indeed, the gospel itself is not just orientated to the next life; it is a programme for bringing about the kingdom of God here on earth in time. The characteristics of this kingdom of God on earth are love, peace and justice. Religion is a private matter on one level but it is also a disclosure about the shape of a truly human world here in time. Religion has a socially prophetic role – to disclose the model of such a society and to do everything it can to encourage the model into being through the responsible agents that are governments, social agencies, science and technology.

It would take too long to develop this understanding of religion and this form of social responsibility that religion has. I have to refer the reader to the social teaching of the church which details this particular understanding of religion as a programme for human and social progress. It is found in the social encyclicals of the Popes from Leo XIII to John Paul II.

I agree with van Vogt that science and technology exist to be major players in human progress, and that they have the major responsibility in moral terms for developing the kind of world all people should inhabit.

While the word technology is relatively new, what it represents is very old, about five million years old. Technology has been around a long time. We tend to forget that. It has gone through many stages. It is still developing. It first came out of man's head in pre-history when he faced his hostile world and sought to make it serve his needs. Technology is as old as religion. In fact both of them were probably born at the same time. And both have had one critical function – the advancement of the human that is in us. They may, of course, define it differently.

Both are in the business of human development and progress. Sometimes they get in each other's way. But the length of their history together tells us the same thing – that they need each other and that human and social progress depend on them both despite their faults, their tensions and their sometimes rivalry.

I suggested at the beginning of this chapter that the question of 'religion or technology?' may be a false one. I think it is. Too often, in human affairs, we set up false opposites. It should not be a question of either religion or technology as the spur for human progress and humanisation. Both are involved in the effort.

A more pertinent question may be whether any real human progress has been achieved over the past technological century. To some, it is the century that produced humankind's greatest wars and the very worst of wars – with their massive destruction made possible by science and technology. Did twentieth-century technology merely 'enlarge our instrumentalities without improving our purposes?'[17] Did twentieth-century technology only serve to make our sin and our selfishness more skilled and more deadly than ever before? And is this the face of the increasingly technological future that lies before us?

I'd like to think not. I believe that twentieth-century technology has given us great gifts especially in medicine. In that century we achieved not only advances in technology but also, despite all the violence, advances in religious spirit, caring and compassion. I am aware of the many social negatives that surround us. But there are great positives too. A simple illustration. The human family has never before had so many effective organisations and instrumentalities of peace and justice and sharing as it has today, nor so many people and agencies committed to bringing about a truly human world. And even the historians of sparse praise will allow this much at least: that today 'the lowliest strata in civilised states may still differ only slightly from barbarians, but above those levels thousands, millions have reached mental and moral levels rarely found among primitive men.'[18]

Why apologise?

Since I started this book the official church has been apologising. It has been apologising, as they say, all over the place. The Pope has just apologised to the Jews and the Bishop of Raphoe has apologised for the child abuse of one of his priests. I presume it is all as genuine as the heart can make it. It is done because it needs to be done. It is also an effort to set the past at rest and to celebrate Jubilee 2000 and start the new millennium with a clean slate and a new heart.

Some apologies remain outstanding. No apology has been made to the priests and nuns and religious brothers throughout the world who have been falsely accused of abuse in various forms. None has been made to those sacrificed to the church's panic and lack of due process. At least I'm aware of none in the public arena. So will there have to be another day of disclosure for them and another day of reckoning for the church? And how will the official church look once again?

It is a sensitive time to be a priest or a religious in the church and one can see in this another reason for the drop in vocations. One sees in this, too, a reason why many priests are settling for a truncated ministry. They want to have as little to do with children as possible. They want to keep women and homosexuals at arm's length. They shy away from counselling and spiritual direction. They are in the business of referral – passing the care of the flock along to others. And all this is happening at a time when the theology of Vatican II is directing them to a more intense involvement in these areas of co-operation, relationship and responsibility.

But why does the church feel it necessary to apologise? Let us leave aside the obvious human factors of embarrassment and public demand and the better factors that are the instincts of natural justice and fair play.

The church apologises because it is a requirement of our religion. We are sinners and we need forgiveness. We need the forgiveness of God and the forgiveness of those we offend. We sin every day and are in constant need of forgiveness. We come out of Jewish roots, and hence are immersed in Jewish theology. One aspect of that theology is the Jubilee year. In our parish churches we see banners proclaiming the year 2000 not as the millennium year but as the Jubilee year.

The Jews of old were required by God to set each 50th year as a Jubilee year. It was a year of forgiveness and of redemption for those in need of it. It concerned issues of land mainly as we see in chapter 25 of the book of Leviticus. In the bible, debt accumulates. And so does sin. As Jesus began his public ministry of preaching and reconciliation, he announced a Jubilee year:

The Spirit of the Lord is upon me,
because he has anointed me
to bring good news to the poor.
He has sent me to proclaim release to the captives
and recovery of sight to the blind,
to let the oppressed go free,
to proclaim the year of the Lord's favour. (Lk. 4:18-19)

When our Lord spoke those words he certainly had their Jewish landed roots in mind. But he also had the accumulated debt and the accumulated sin of humankind in mind. Forgiveness would be central to his mission. We have a need to seek forgiveness and a hope that those we offend will give it since they too are sinners. It is in that spirit, I think, that the church celebrates the Jubilee. It is with that hope of forgiveness that the church apologises today. It may bring some a form of healing. It may bring the public a form of closure. But I use these overused words of healing and closure very tenuously. Why?

I'm not sure of the effectiveness of the church's apologies and its cry for forgiveness. An effective apology requires that it be accepted by the offended party. I'm not sure that this has happened – or ever will happen – with some of the church's victims. I'm not sure, for example, that in the matter of the Jewish Holocaust the living can speak for the dead. I'm not sure, from the newspaper reports of court cases, that all the victims of child sexual abuse will forgive their penitent tormentors. I'm not sure that the theology of the church can allow the church to be so non-offensive to some persons and groups that apologies of one kind or another will never again be demanded of the church. What do I mean by that?

The passion story and the gospel of St John and the Acts of the Apostles have, as a recurring negative, the phrase 'the Jews.' There is a minority opinion within the church, and a stronger view outside it, that these and similar negative words and attitudes continue to give Christian scripture an anti-Jewish flavour and should be changed. Only in that practical way can Christian anti-Semitism be removed. And only such actions will give substance to our apology to the Jewish people and put reality into the symbolism of the Pope's visit to the western wall in Jerusalem and to the written apology he placed in it. In a similar way, the Old Testament (the Jewish scriptures) has the recurring negative 'the Gentiles.' These are 'the pagans who know not God'. They are us! Should these Jewish scriptures also be changed?

How much of every religion's scripture needs to be changed, and how could this be done, in order to remove what some see as the *real* religious sources of bias and prejudice? But even if the scriptural basis of bigotry were gone, the flawed human heart remains. It is the Lord who said wisely:

> Listen and understand: it is not what goes into the mouth that defiles a person, but it is what comes out of the mouth that defiles ... Do you not see that whatever goes into the mouth enters the stomach, and goes out into the sewer? But what comes out of the mouth proceeds from the heart, and this is what defiles. For out of the heart come evil intentions, murder, adultery, fornication, theft, false witness, slander. These are what defile a person ... (Mt 15:10-20)

The origin of all sin, including bias and bigotry, is not in scripture but in the human heart. It is the heart that needs healing.

What may be more troublesome than apology, or the issue of ways and means in apology, is the knowledge that it may happen again. All the apologies in the world are no guarantee that history will not repeat itself. In fact, it does. Sin remains in the human condition even if each generation is a new generation and sees itself as pristine. Each generation is new on the stage of life but its temptations and propensities are those of the antecedent generations. These temptations and propensities will seek expression. Pre-warnings and safeguards are, of course, in place now as a result of our recent history. But absolute sanitation and security are not.

So, what's the point in apologising? Well, often it's the only thing we can do, and all that we can do. In my experience, an apology is sometimes all that the offended person is looking for. We see victims of injustice and people bereaved by violence on TV whose lament is: 'No one ever apologised to us.' I suppose in terms of human solidarity (and Christian solidarity and national solidarity) we can apologise for the past and even for what will occur in the as yet unknown future.

And we can apologise and go on apologising in the hope that the development of a reflexive attitude of apology in us may lessen the likelihood of our offending others again. And I imagine that an apologetic society is a society well on the road to becoming properly human and humane. Those are some answers I give to the question: What's the point in apologising?

But in the last analysis, and for the Christian, I think we apologise and we seek forgiveness and we offer forgiveness because Forgiveness is a name for our God.

Why the anti-Semitic attitude?

I believe that a Jewish person could answer this question much better than I. However, the full question asked is this: 'Why, over the centuries, did the church adopt such anti-Semitic attitudes especially with the belief that Jesus was born a Jew himself?' Those who ask this question want the church, not Jewish people, to answer.

We touched on aspects of this question in the previous chapter. I think that the sources of Christian anti-Semitism may be traced to the rejection of Jesus by his own people, to his death, to the reaction of his followers to those events, to the subsequent persecution of the church by the Jews in Jerusalem, and to the excommunication of Jesus' followers from Judaism.

I say these are sources. Of themselves they were not anti-Semitic actions or attitudes since the parties involved on both sides were Semites (i.e. Jews). Christian anti-Semitism as a social phenomenon comes much later. Anti-Semitism does not begin with the age of Christ. Forms of anti-Semitism existed before Christianity and outside of Christianity. They still do. Very much so.

The sources of Christian anti-Semitism are found in the New Testament writings – in the gospels, in John and in the Acts of the Apostles. Reading the gospels, we are conscious of the antagonism of 'the Jews' (a recurring phrase) and of most of the Jewish religious establishment to Jesus and to his teachings and to his claims. John strikes me as more critical of the Jewish rejection of Jesus than any of the others. And I suspect this comes partly from his intense love of and personal commitment to Christ.

The Acts of the Apostles gives us a picture of the early church and its struggles. Its struggles are with the Jews who persecute it. It is a church that is heroic and full of grace from our point of view. However, if you were a dedicated Jew what would you make of some of the lines in Peter's Pentecostal speech, lines that seem to disparage your Jewish religion and blame you for the death of Jesus? Here is a sample. I have italicised the relevant lines:

> You that are Israelites, listen to what I have to say: Jesus of Nazareth, a man attested to you by God with deeds of power, wonders and signs that God did through him among you, as you yourselves know – this man, handed over to you according to the definite plan and foreknowledge of God, *you crucified and killed by the hands of those outside the law.* But God raised him up ... Therefore let the entire house of Israel know with certainty that God has made him both Lord and Messiah, this Jesus *whom you crucified.'* (Acts 2:22-36)

Peter directly involves 'Israelites,' i.e. the Jews, in the killing of Jesus and insults the Jews further by referring to their use of people outside the law (i.e. Gentiles, the unclean) in his death. These were the Roman authorities.

Now, of course, the purpose of Peter's speech is not to condemn the Jews. He loves them. He is one of them. He wants to convert them to Jesus as the Messiah and Lord who fulfils the Jewish promises made by God. That is why he makes the allowance that Jesus died 'according to the definite plan and foreknowledge of God.'

In Peter's next speech we have the same issue of the Jews and Jesus' death. Instead of italicising the blaming lines I'll highlight the excusing lines:

> The God of Abraham, the God of Isaac, and the God of Jacob, the God of our ancestors has glorified his servant Jesus, whom you handed over and rejected in the presence of Pilate, though he had decided to release him ... you killed the Author of life, whom God raised from the dead ... *I know that you acted in ignorance, as did also your rulers.* (Acts 3:13-17)

If Peter intended to pin Jesus' death exclusively or primarily on the Jews he would not talk of our Lord being delivered to the cross 'according to the definite plan and foreknowledge of God' nor would he tell the Jews that they 'acted out of ignorance'. Peter, like all the apostles, is perfectly aware of the theological fact that Jesus was killed by *our* sins, that 'Christ died for our sins.' (1 Cor. 15:3)

The Acts of the Apostles goes on to record various incidents in which the apostles and Christians are persecuted by the Jewish establishment for preaching the name of Jesus. It is an on-going persecution and it certainly cemented antagonism between the two camps. The persecution is confined to Palestine and mostly to Jerusalem where the Jewish authorities held a measure of power within the Roman empire. Many of the difficulties of the early Christians vis-à-vis the established Jewish religion are mentioned in the first chapter of Henry Chadwick's classic work, *The Early Church*.[19]

The early Christians in Jerusalem were Jews themselves and they continued to attend synagogue and observe Jewish ritual. Our Lord had foretold that they would be persecuted in the synagogues, and so it happened eventually. They were not known as Christians but as Jews who followed 'the Nazorean.' The antagonism reached a head and they were excommunicated from the synagogues. Around the years 85 to 90 AD at Jamnia 'the Nazoreans' were cursed, formally and religiously, by the assembled rabbis and named heretics. This action likely drove the two sides completely apart and we can assume that it played a part in later Christian anti-Semitism.

The sources of Christian anti-Semitism, then, lie in the death of Jesus, the Jewish persecution of the early church, the rejection of Christ and the apostles' preaching by the vast majority of the Jewish people in Israel, the words of Peter and the apostles, and the excommunication from official Judaism of the followers of Jesus. But how did this translate itself into the full-blown Christian anti-Semitism that pockmarks European history? And why has it been so persistent and so ugly that the Pope goes to the western wall in Jerusalem and apologises in what may be for him the most symbolic gesture of his pontificate?

I don't know. But neither do I understand how an intelligent reading of the New Testament writings would lead people to put the emphasis in the wrong places and on the wrong lines and to miss the intense desire that the apostles showed for the acceptance of Christ by his own people. I cannot see how even the slightest understanding of the death of Jesus as the great salvation event of history should lead people to anti-Semitism. We are told over and over in the New Testament, as we are in the church and in our catechisms, that Christ died for our sins and that it was the sins of humanity that put him on the cross. Christ was killed by our sins, not by the Jews. Without sin there would be no death of Christ. Nor can I quite understand why the persecution of the small 'Jewish' church in Palestine should lead to 2000 years of anti-Semitism among the descendants of the vast 'Hellenistic' church everywhere else outside of Palestine.

I cannot understand how any Christian in any age would not feel kinship with the Jews who are God's chosen people, who kept faith in the one God when all others about them worshipped idols, who prepared the way of salvation for us, who gave us the Messiah, and Our Lady and St Joseph and all the apostles as well as most of the 'Christian' (they are Jewish) names with which we were baptised and by which we are known to one and all. We are all, in the words of Pius XI, spiritual Semites. Our most important ancestry is rooted beyond Irish history and beyond the Celts in Judaism itself.

On the other hand, I do understand anti-Semitism (and all the other racisms of the world) as an expression of human sinfulness. Sin is the theological name for anti-Semitism as it is for all forms of hatred. I realise that awful sermons must have been preached over the generations, sermons that stirred up religious hatred of the Jews, sermons that caused Christians – in one historical instance in eastern Europe – to rush out of church on Good Friday and kill Jews in their ghetto. I know that economic jealousy has played its part too and that politicians and nationalisms made names and gains out of their anti-Jewish attitudes.

I realise full well that our sin-prone human nature loves to look for enemies and to name them, that we waste time discriminating between who's in and who's out in our little world, that we have a weakness for naming scapegoats and fingering others, that we build psychological walls and fences based on all the wrong things like money, colour of skin, racial type, ethnic origin, sexuality, class and religion. Sometimes we even build concentration camps. And worse, extermination camps. And once upon a time in Europe some of us did.

Is the church an ethically inferior institution?

Those of us who are the older generation in the church probably never dreamed that such a question as this could ever be asked. We were born in the church. Many of us may have spent our lives promoting and spreading the church. We have defended the church. We have spoken for it. We have written for it. We have been in love with it. We have grown old with it.

Love of the church was instilled into us from childhood. The kind of church history we read told of a good and a great church. The church went about its business of making us holy and doing good to all and sundry. We accepted that readily. After all, it was founded by Christ and is led by the Holy Spirit. We marvelled at its many saints and wondered with a pious jealousy if we might not become one of them ourselves. Men and women went overseas in their thousands to extend the church, and each of us wondered if we too might not be graced with a vocation. The church had many enemies and critics but they were all outside the walls.

Now, of course, people such as priests who had to study the church in some depth were aware of some of the more human side of the church's history. But the average parishioner was unaware of the blotches and the stains. He and she went from strength to strength in admiration of the church. They were fed a constant diet of the church glorious and triumphant. When the first child abuse stories broke, they were upset. When they became a pattern, they were humiliated. When the cover-ups of the church authorities became known, they were devastated.

On a purely human level, there is nothing unusual about the church trying to hide its soiled linen. Every institution in the world does it. Even every family. And every one of us. The big institutions spend big money on self-promotion and on public relations and on image. Among their highest paid employees are their lawyers and their 'damage limitation' experts. I take it as a measure of the church's honesty and even innocence that it did not have in the past, generally speaking, such experts. I would like to think that the church believed there was no need for them because there was nothing major to hide. That is a measure of how unexpected the number of the scandals was.

And yet we now know that at least some bishops were aware of major problems and did nothing to resolve them. And common sense indicates that an international church of one billion members ought to expect sins and scandals based on the sheer numbers of clergy and faithful, and on the different cultures and traditions they come out of. Jesus told us there would always be scandals. One could say that the church leadership was at least aware of the lessons of history and therefore ought to have had pre-emptive measures in place. And one could say that the church should have been all the more alert to the possibility of moral laxity in our time since it is an age characterised by sexual revolution and change.

One could say that there was no strong moral guidance in the drifting church of the 1960s and 1970s and that some negative moral fallout ought to have been expected from those decades by the authorities. In fact, the post-Vatican II church was in a kind of moral free-fall at that time as I remember it. All of those points may help to explain the charge of incompetence against church authorities.

One could also say, and critics do, that the church was very aware of the behaviour of its clergy but swept it under the carpet. In this scenario, the church showed a serious lack of justice and of concern for victims. It did not act until it was forced to act by the outcry of the people and the initiative of the civil authorities. It is *this* that alarms at least some people the most. When you add that to the church's position as traditional moral guide and its stress on its divine right to be humankind's authentic moral teacher, the combination makes the church look all the more ethically deficient. Which is why it has lost its moral leadership with this generation and why it may have to settle for a much lesser moral influence on future generations.

Has it lost more? Is it in fact, as suggested by our questioner, an ethically inferior institution when its behaviour is critiqued by commonly held moral standards? Even by so-called secular standards?

Is it ethically inferior to, say, a modern western democratic government or to a major medical or charitable association? The church looks great morally on paper. But what about in practice? Again we come up against the issue of theological connections and disconnections. The church's recent apologies cover not just individual victimisations but some historical moral outrages as well. The apologies cover not only the present but range through the church's history. This only adds to the weight of disconnection.

How does one respond to these facts and to our question? I do not know if any institution would fare any better morally if it had a 2000-year history like the church. That is not an excuse. It's an observation. That long a history has to be judged by its own contemporary standards, not by the enlightened hindsight of a 21st-century moral standard. And when we look at the 20th century, the century all of us lived in, I think it fair to say that while it was a century of progress it was also one of horrific wars, genocides and human violations and that the weight of its sin and the burden of its guilt lie with institutions other than the church. But this is only a poor excuse to many outside critics and cold comfort to younger Catholics who want to love the church and whose idealism is struggling to remain intact.

Church history is not just the 1990s. It is wider than the past decade and deeper than the apologies that have had to be made. Absent from the present autopsy on the church is its huge history of grace and achievement, i.e. of social ethics realised. The past 2000 years have shown us a church whose pilgrim passage is much more than the sum of its sin. Strange how we Irish especially should gather at the wake of the church and not recount any of its virtues and achievements when Irish funerals so readily list the virtues and achievements of even the lowliest corpse in the land.

I do not need a library, nor will I ask you to read church history, to find some representative illustrations of the church's story of achievement and of grace. All I have to do is walk around an Irish town and the story is written on its stones. In my sacred place, Athenry, there is the ruined abbey where monks transcribed the scriptures and fashioned the stained glass windows that taught us Irish about God and goodness and our relationships with him and among ourselves. That abbey and those monks remind me of earlier abbeys and monks who rekindled civilisation in Europe ('saved it,' according to Thomas Cahill) after the Dark Ages.

In that abbey is the chancel where the sinner and the unjustly accused and the poor (who were the scapegoat of fashion then) found sanctuary from lord and sheriff. In the abbey grounds are the library ruins and the now disappeared dormitories that introduced Connacht in the 1600s to the exciting world of university education thanks to Rome. In the town square is the stone cross of the Crucified that named my street of birth and that pledged the inviolability of contracts and oaths, and thereby secured peace in the community. In Leonard's lawn is the Spital Gate in the town walls that led to the leprosarium. The slits in the walls near that particular gate were put there, it is believed, not for defensive reasons but so that our people could pass food and compassion to the most unfortunate of their era, the lepers. Those slits are an expression in stone of the effectiveness of church teaching back then and of the fearlessness of the taught who, in risking contact with the lepers, risked a slow and rotting death.

Within that walled town are so many expressions of humanity, generated by a caring and graced church. Within that walled town are my reminders that the great western institutions that are library and hospital and hostel and university education are the graces and the gifts to us of that church we nowadays too readily want to wake.

And there are other gifts of the church – the deeply satisfying spiritual paths taught by our saints and mystics that are step-by-step guides to inner peace and proven union with the Lord. How deeply would they not calm and connect with God the anxious and the suicidal among our young people! There are, too, the gifted insights from the church's moral tradition that played their part in the forging of such majestic civil charters as the Magna Carta and the modern democratic constitution.

We, of the older church, haven't told the story to this generation. We haven't passed on the church's gifted history or the naming of its treasures and how valuable they could be to the hurt and hollow modern soul. We have forgotten what the liturgy calls the *anamnesis* of our faith – that we remember; that we are a people who are commanded by Jesus to remember; that we remember what the Lord did on earth; that we remember what his church has done for the world. We need only a small intelligence and an unbiased heart to appreciate how dark it all was before he came, and how impoverished humanity might have remained without the fellowship and the inventiveness and the heart of the church down all the years.

Church conformity or loyalty to Jesus?

There is a tendency among Catholics to live more and more with less and less connection with the church. It is happening, of course, with the so-called à la carte Catholics. But it is happening with the young and middle generations too.

So many are becoming Catholics with what I call formal church limits. They want some sacraments from the church. They want the Mass – when they want it. They do not want spiritual direction because they believe the church has shown little competence in that area in recent generations. They want almost no contact with officialdom and church authority. It has spoken too strongly and too wrongly in the past especially on sex and censorship. It has burdened them in the past with guilt and disappointed them in the present with its sin and its confusion.

I see all but the elderly putting distance into their relationship with the church and I suspect it is the start of a European style Catholicism. I do not think that Catholics will ever again be immersed in the church the way they used to be. They are the ones who are heralding the future of the Irish church as one of concentric circles, each outer circle representing an increasing distance from the centre.

The logical outcome of this distancing may be a quiet form of Protestantism if one wishes to call it that. I read it as an increasingly privatised Catholicism on the way to becoming a privatised religion. Others may praise it for its self-definition. Perhaps they see it as Jesus finally coming to the centre of a believer's life and being 'the only thing that matters' with the church as a sometimes helpful adjunct or a sometimes unhelpful pest. In the end of the day it all comes down to God and the individual.

The recent deficiencies of the church no doubt have helped to lessen its influence with its members. The deficiencies are, indeed, the individual clerical abuses and victimisations we saw in the media but they are also the historical exposés involving church authority. It may be the sins of the leadership and the institutional lapses that mostly lessen the church's attractiveness for these Catholics. This has been the case historically in Europe and it may well be the case today in Ireland.

Other institutional expressions also help to make the church less attractive to believers and help create the distance. I've mentioned elsewhere the pomp and the deference and the titles of popes, cardinals, and bishops. These things tend to demand an obsequious mentality of men and women who, to the contrary, will not tolerate such today and who are told in scripture that they are all equal in Christ and that they are graced with 'the glorious freedom of the children of God.' (Rom 8:21)

These people are also the Catholics who, in trying to connect with God and Jesus, sometimes feel that they have to run the gauntlet or engage in a kind of obstacle course with the church in order to find grace or to stay in grace. The obstacle course has two tiers.

First, there is church authority and its many layers. One is reminded of the TV movie, *Immigrants,* in which a Swedish man hopes that the New World will be a place where he will be free of kings, princes, lords, sheriffs, bailiffs, archbishops, bishops and pastors. Too many authorities stand between him and his dreams and between him and his relationship with God. Second, there is the centralist channelling of grace by the church, and the ritualisation and detailed regulations that surround grace. The church controls the channels of grace that are called word and sacrament.

Both of these layers seem to be so widespread and so detailed as to make the believer's approach to God and grace an obstacle course or a minefield. One may add to these two layers another layer or obstacle. And that is the mindset of the local church – the believer's bishop or local parish clergy – whose authority can pressure one's conscience – and it has – into justifying an immoral silence or an immoral boycott and almost everything else in between. These several layers strike many contemporary Catholics as obstacles for them in their quest for God. They also create distance. One can so easily become a religious outsider in one's own church.

Obviously, this over-institutionalisation of authority and its trenchant control of grace has led to 'ruptures' in the Christian church over the years. The Great Schism and the Reformation are, in part, re-actions to it. Vatican II has attempted to redress the over-institutionalisation in so far as the council felt it could. There is a change of language and of sentiment. Authority is defined as a service. Control is a charism. But the full vigour of authority and centralisation remains. Non-Catholic believers say the council did not go far enough and that Christian unity in any substantive sense will remain a far distant dream because of these very issues of authority and the control of grace.

It is against this background of institutionalisation and control, and in the context of the increased personal freedom and self-direction of people today, that I see so many Catholics remaining in the church while living at an emotional and theological distance from it. It is an entirely new religious phenomenon in Irish history. I believe it will only increase. It has created a question in many Catholic minds: church conformity or loyalty to Jesus?

I understand this to mean: Do I bypass much of the authority and control of the church over God, grace and me and, instead, do I prioritise my conscience, the plain word of God, free access to grace, and dependence on the 'Spirit dwelling in you.' (Rom 8:11)? And will I do all this and still remain within the church? I just cannot remain centred on the church the way I used to be.

I think the official church is partly responsible for setting up this dilemma for Catholics and I doubt that Vatican II properly addressed it. It is new to Ireland. It is old hat on the Continent.

All authoritarian institutions, religious and secular, are faced with the same dilemma today. History has hurt them. History has been moving for a long time in the direction of democracy and personal freedom. It has been moving in the direction of personalism and self-determination. The present long span of peace and the economy of the west have helped and encouraged the dilemma. People want greater control of their lives and the right to shape their lives freely. This is especially true in regard to life's key ingredients. Religion, one's relationship with God, is one such key ingredient.

The church, they feel, has not made appropriate adjustments. On the contrary, the Pope regards the western world to be out on a limb, overboard on capitalism, consumerism, democracy, self-interest and personal autonomy. He looks to Asia and Africa. But the truth is that they too seem to be yearning for the same standards of wealth, consumerism, autonomy and self-determination. Lyndon Johnson once said, 'Let's face it: they all want what we have.'

The church, they feel, continues to harp on its authority. It still wants to control everything down to the last letter of scriptural interpretation and the last ritualised detail of grace. It appears to many contemporary Catholics that the church stands in the way between God and grace and them. I think the phenomenon of the Catholic in the church but distanced from it will only increase in the foreseeable future.

The church is aware of the dilemma it is in (though it appears to take little responsibility for creating it) and that many of its members are in. Its responses vary. Its official theology has gone back to stressing the unity of Jesus and the church, their mutual love, even their interchangeability, in the hope that this will remove the 'either or' mentality expressed in our question. Theologians have come up with 'models' of church that are more attractive than the one institutional model we are all familiar with. The church may be experienced as an institution but it can also be experienced as a servant community, as a community gathered around the word of God, as the eucharistic community, as the prophetic community, and as the community that heralds the Good News of Jesus.

John Paul II is criticised for responding to our question with nothing better than re-statements of authority and obedience. That is partly true. But his personal life and his pastoral travels may be his way of expressing church in other ways such as social builder and prophetic voice for justice and peace.

Whatever the responses, many Catholics will remain in the church but with, if we may say so, Protestant caution in their theology and democratic components in their value system. Neither label means much to them. They are educated, self-determining and believing followers of Jesus. Their heads are full of the cautions triggered by institutional religious history and by the limitations of religious leaders. They live out of the fact that trust has been betrayed and that apology has had to be made. There is scepticism of the institution on their faces. They are children of democracy and of equal rights and of personal responsibility before God. To them, no religion has an advantage with God over another. No religion is better than any other. They have experienced the triumphalist church as unChristian. They have experienced sectarianism as the root of much evil in their land and an insult to God. They have let the church be their teacher and guide for too long and with little spiritual return on their investment. They look at the larger canvas of religion: that we are all God's children and that his Son died for all without exception.

And so, the church as institution and as religious authority and as intrepid controller of grace finds little love with them and is of no unusual value to their personal, family, and daily lives. They use the parish church for life's markers such as weddings and first communions and funerals because it is there and because of cultural requirement and tradition. They use it for baptism and eucharist and any other things useful to their personal faith. But they find no great spirituality there. They don't really expect to. Insight and grace, like God, are being found in other places.

Parish life could in the future fade into a European landscape of churches as tourist stops. If that happens it will mean that these Catholics will have 'gone the distance,' that their faith will have become a basically unchurched thing, a private church of the heart.

If these Catholics are to remain connected with the church at a deeper level, and if the 'either-or' of our question is to become 'both' – both church and Jesus, as it should – the quality of the local priest may be the determining factor. I believe he is the key player in the question we are dealing with here.

On a day-to-day level, people have no dealings with Pope, cardinal, archbishop or bishop. And most official theology never crosses their path or filters down into their concerns. It is the local priest who is the official church for them in practical terms. Surely he can be – as many already are – the sensitive, servant, pastoral church to them too. I think he is absolutely critical to what happens to these Catholics in their relationship with the institutional church in the years ahead. At the moment, these Catholics are polite but sceptical, still joined to the church but cautious, unfulfilled and at a distance from it. The Lord and not the church is at the centre of their religion. It should always have been that way, of course. But there must be room for others too. Who will be allowed with Christ into their hearts? It's still an open question.

For these people, having the Lord at the centre, and the official church scarcely in the background, has been a difficult journey. It has meant breaking familiar ties and turning backs on their grandparents' religious set-pieces. They simply needed a more personal relationship with their Lord given the times that are in it. They did not set out with distance from the church as a goal. But that's where they've arrived at. Of course, having Jesus at the centre is where he always should have been. That is the goal of salvation history. And for them to have shaped so much of this centring is also to be part of the times that are in it. It is the age of self-determination and personal responsibility.

For the church, these people are a bottom line. And they are a prophetic challenge. They are an expression of the distance that exists between the church and the modern mindset. It is a distance not all of the church's making by any means. It is a distance created by secular education and democracy, by self-determination and personalism. It is a distance created by relative wealth, consumerism and the relentless invasion by media of the European lifestyle and its values.

But it also a distance created by the lack of adult religious education, close church communities, one-on-one Christian exchange and honest interfacing such as existed in the early church. It is a distance created by the sins and the need for apology, by the authoritarianism and the institutionalisation of just about every aspect of religion; a distance created by the control and the clericalism and the pomp and the spiritual poverty; a distance created by the church's vision and its actual performance on the ground.

These people are indeed children of their culture; but they are also an expression of the church's own theology of disconnection and failed translation.

Why are the media so hostile to the church?

The question assumes that the Irish media are very hostile to the church. I don't find the media to be all that hostile at the moment. They have moved from being considerably hostile in the recent past to adopting a posture somewhere between the cautionary and the dismissive in relation to the church.

Certainly, media hostility to the church was pronounced in the past decade. There was at times a sort of feeding frenzy about the media during those years in relation to the Catholic Church's difficulties. At the same time, one cannot avoid the fact that the church provided the grounds for much of the hostility and that its past shortcomings justify a certain media caution now in relation to it. One reaps what one sows, according to scripture.

One finds an occasional hostile piece nowadays but it's very tired stuff, nothing better than a parody or the flailing of a dead horse by an equally dead imagination. The personal psychology of the author of such a hackneyed piece is one that is stuck in perpetual adolescence. With time one learns what to expect from whom in the media. That observation applies anywhere in the world, not just in Ireland.

Why were Irish media hostile to the church in the 1990s? I'm sure there was more than one reason. I'll give you a few possible ones. And I'll work from the bottom up.

Irish media, like media everywhere, have their quota of unethical hacks. I use 'hack' here not to describe the trusty foot soldier of the media world but to describe the lazy journalist who cuts corners, especially ethical corners, to get his or her story or to manufacture one. He and she did unjustifiable damage to church members and thereby to the church in general. These journalists bother me in the sense that they got away with it. They don't bother me in the sense that there are hacks and cowboys in every walk of life including my own.

Then there's the issue of the human nature of the journalist himself and herself. The people who incarnate the media are, quite naturally, a cross-section of society. They are men and women with weaknesses and limitations. They are not gods. They are as much the children of Adam as any of us. And they are just as flawed in their judgements, as quick in their condemnations and as hassled and as hurried to make copy and meet deadlines. Yet the TV image and the printed word come across to us as messages of dispassionate objectivity and care. They lend the journalist and the reporter an aura of near infallibility. The public must school itself in the fact that a news story is not an exercise in scholarship, much less in infallibility.

Democracy, worthy of the name, requires a high degree of intellectual and moral maturity in the people who 'generate' the news and in those who 'consume' it. Such maturity is required if a democratic society and its media are to be honest, humane and civil; just, fair and compassionate. I don't think this kind of maturity exists in any great measure among many of us and its absence in at least some media reporting on the church in the 1990s was manifest.

There will always be people in the media who are suspicious of the church as they are of all institutions and establishments. (Ironically, the media are one of the great institutions and establishments of the day). There always have been. It goes with the territory. There is something of the avenging prophet in the psychology of the journalist and the reporter. They need to see themselves as knights in shining armour, uncoverers of evil, defenders of the little guy and the moral scourge of the power-broker. That is fine in itself. But it can lead to other things. It can lead to a sense of personal Godlikeness and to a lack of objectivity, humanity and fair play. I believe it did, to a degree, in the 1990s hostility to the church. It is that phrase 'to a degree' that, in news coverage, makes all the difference.

It is of some clinical interest that the journalist and the reporter have taken over the pulpit of the bishop and the priest and are always in danger of purveying the faults they condemned in them – snobbery, superiority, easy condemnation and cant. One rather blind dogmatism should not be replaced by another rather blind dogmatism.

Journalists, for all their pretentions, are just like the rest of us. They are tempted to get back at those who hurt them, to get back at the church. The hurt may be something from schooldays, maybe nothing more personal than the all-pervading clerical influence that we all suffered under in our education and early life.

Or at issue may be the accumulated jealousy of the years when the clergy beat out the journalists for the ear, mind and heart of the people. The clergy always ranked above the journalists in the polls of the most trustworthy in the past. Or at issue may be the kinship media people feel they have with the creative writers who felt the scourge of state and church censorship in the past. In this psychology, the world of the media may be expected to show hostility to the church as occasion allows. The 1990s allowed it. No doubt the media of the 1990s contained several players who were (and still are) in the business of sanitising the old Ireland and fashioning the new one. As we saw in a previous chapter, their great obstacle was and still is the Catholic Church. Accordingly, the church came in for as great a hammering as these people could give it. That, too, accounts for some of the media hostility to the church.

But for me, at any rate, there is another side to this coin and it is by a long stretch the more cogent side in any discussion of media hostility to the church in the 1990s. Those of us who trained in communications learned a few simple rules of reportage. First, is there a story? Second, what are the *facts*? Third, how (i.e. angle, slant, etc.) – and sometimes when – does one report it?

In the 1990s the church provided the story. The facts were reported by the media as best they were able to uncover them. It is the third rule alone that should generate any discussion in relation to media hostility in the 1990s. Facts have to be organised, and this involves selectivity – and honest judgement. The resulting story is expected by the public to be balanced and unbiased. Some pieces I read in the 1990s were not, and maybe for one of the reasons I listed already and maybe also because of the stonewalling and confusion of the church authorities themselves. All in all, I suspect that most reporters did the best they could with the ever-erupting scene of the 1990s and that the bishops didn't know how to respond or what was going to hit them next.

There may be a wider context into which this sad story of the 1990s sin and confusion fits, and of which it is only one part. The wider context is the one I have been suggesting in other chapters with regard to such phenomena as the à la carte Catholic, the 'concentric' Catholic, the modern mindset, the absence of adult catechesis and mature, reflected-upon faith and morality generally in the church of the modern era. To me the church has been limping along with a wide-ranging theology of disconnection and failed translation. Vatican II, in retrospect, may not have been an adequate council for the challenges and tasks that had accumulated over several centuries and that confronted it. And we, the national and local churches, never got up to speed with its best insights anyway. I find it all encapsulated in the image of my own bishop, a cardinal, stepping off the plane in 1965 and telling the assembled media, 'Two words – no change.' Even I, as a young curate then, knew we were in for trouble.

And so, I tell myself, rightly or wrongly, that from the pastoral and socio-cultural standpoints the sad events of the 1990s merely breached the dam of Irish religion that was going to burst sooner or later, one way or another.

Explain the Second Coming of Christ

The first coming of Christ was his birth in Bethlehem. The second coming of Christ is his return near the end of history to bring it to a close. We refer to it in the Creed at Sunday Mass when we say, 'He will come again in glory to judge the living and the dead.'

The phrase 'second coming' is not itself found in the bible. It is a popular phrase that evangelical Christians use today. It is a reflection of the scriptures which speak of Christ's 'coming again' (Jn 14:3) and his 'appearance a second time.' (Heb 9:28)

Since Christ comes many times and in many ways to people in every generation, and since we meet him every day in word and sacrament, many Catholic scholars prefer to use the words 'final coming' rather than 'second coming'.

The final coming of Christ is a stage in the *parousia,* a Greek word which means the consummation of history in God. All history has been, and is even now, moving toward its appointed culmination in Christ. It is moving towards its final stage and it is moving to its judgement. The judgement will be severe on some of its aspects and on some of its actors but serene and blessed for others.

Part of the *parousia* will be the vindication of Christ as the servant of history and the saviour of our personal histories, and he will be shown, as befits his saving work and saving death, in his glory. He will be revealed to all as 'the King of kings and the Lord of lords' (Rev 19:16), as the lord of history, life and love.

Is the final coming in this life or in the next? It is in this life, in time as we know it, and in history. When will it happen? At the end. You may have noticed that many were expecting the Lord's final coming on the eve of the new millennium. Many were expecting the Lord to appear in Jerusalem. You saw that on TV. You may have noticed that the official church and the scholars paid no attention to those who were forecasting the final coming at that time. There are people all over the world who insist on forecasting the day and the hour of the Lord's arrival. They've been doing this for 2000 years and they will continue to do so.

But they ignore the words of Jesus himself: 'But about the day and hour no one knows, neither the angels of heaven, nor the Son, but only the Father.' (Mt 24:36) And they ignore the words of St Peter who said we should not waste our time making useless prognostications. Instead, we should spend the time becoming 'holy in your conduct and devotion' and in that way we may even 'hasten' the final coming. (See 2 Pt 11-12)

Did Our Lord really mean it when he said that even he, the Son of God, didn't know the day or the hour of his final coming? Yes. How are we to understand that apparent ignorance if he was divine? A few scholars think that in this instance God the Father did not permit Jesus to reveal the time of the final coming and that is why he answered as he did. Most scholars, however, say that Jesus spoke these words out of the limits imposed on him by his human nature. Jesus was indeed truly God and truly man but we need to remember that his human nature was at least as engaged as his divine nature when he walked among us.

That is why the gospels can sometimes show Jesus knowing things only God could know and sometimes asking questions as a genuine seeker of knowledge. That is what he was doing when he was lost in the temple for three days. He spent the time asking questions. After this temple event we read in Luke's gospel that he went home to Nazareth with his parents where 'Jesus, *increased in wisdom* and in years, and in divine and human favour.' (2:52) The interaction of the divine and the human knowledge of Jesus is something we cannot fully understand.

Instead of wasting our time making prognostications about the timing of the end, the Lord wants us to concentrate on the gospel and centre our hearts on his. If we do, we need have no fear of judgement or of his final coming but can wait for it joyfully. When the Lord comes again we will be found ready and he will be delighted to meet us with open arms:

> When the Son of Man comes in his glory, and all the angels with him, then he will sit on the throne of his glory. All the

nations will be gathered before him, and he will separate people one from another as a shepherd separates the sheep from the goats, and he will put the sheep at his right hand and the goats at the left. Then the king [Jesus] will say to those at his right hand, 'Come, you that are blessed by my Father, inherit the kingdom prepared for you from the foundation of the world.' (Mt 25:31-34)

What is the future of the church?

There are two versions of the church's future in Ireland. Both seem to be saying basically the same thing. I hear the first version many times on TV talk shows and in the press. It is this: The Catholic Church is in crisis. It is disappearing in terms of both membership and influence. It is not addressing its critical problems and it will continue to wither away.

The second version of the church's future is the one I hear all the time from priests. It is this: The official church is battening down the hatches and steering ahead in a purely survival mode. It expects to become a smaller church in numbers and in influence, and it has accepted this sparse future without putting up a fight because the leadership lacks vision and heart.

Even though the two estimates are alike there is one big difference. The secular estimate believes that the church could eventually disappear altogether. The religious estimate believes that this can never happen. The church has survived many crises in its long history. The official church is fully confident of survival because it believes in the promise of Jesus to Simon Peter: 'And I tell you, you are Peter, and on this rock I will build my church, and the gates of Hades will not prevail against it.' (Mt 16:18)

I am as confident as the bishops that the Irish church will survive. And like them I suspect it will be a smaller church in numbers and in influence. But I reject any defeatist attitude, if there is one, which infers that decline must inevitably happen. The Catholic Church in Ireland does not *have* to become smaller in numbers or in influence. (Why not a new Pentecost and a new evangelisation?) But it will become smaller if its leadership follows the theology it seems to be following at the moment. It is called the theology of the remnant. What is the theology of the remnant?

The theology of the remnant is the conviction that the church has fallen on bad times. It is represented by a faithful core or the faithful few. It will not be destroyed but will survive despite its trials. That's the good point. However, the same theology assumes that most members will fall away and that there is something of the inevitable in this mass defection. The paradigm, or original model, for this is found in the book of Jeremiah (24:1-10). A remnant of Israel passes through the purifying experience of exile and becomes the new Israel loved of God.

In parallel, the official church sees itself passing through a similar experience in Ireland because of the sins and the scandals *and* the turning away of many of the people from God to the false gods of materialism, greed, consumerism and empty sophistication. The Irish church will emerge from the fire as a more faithful but less numerous people of God. In the remnant theology the future numbers of the church do not matter – the quality of the remaining members or 'true believers' does.

There are similar remnant theologies in the Old Testament books of Amos, Micah, and Ezekiel. In the New Testament, Paul is pleased that a remnant of his own Jewish people has accepted the grace of Christ. (See Rom 11:5) The Book of Revelation (or Apocalypse) is written to a faithful remnant – all that was left of the great apostolic church – as the first century A.D. came to a close. And even Jesus seems to reflect the remnant mentality on several occasions, as when he speaks of his 'little flock.' (Lk 12:32) and when he tells us to 'Enter through the narrow gate, for the gate is wide and the road is easy that leads to destruction, and there are many who take it. For the gate is narrow and the road is hard that leads to life, and there are few who find it.' (Mt 7:13-14)

So, if the bishops have battened down the hatches and adopted the theology of the remnant, they have good biblical precedents to go by. However, I question the appropriateness of a remnant theology in our Irish circumstances. I do not believe it is the right pastoral response for the start of a new millennium. It is clearly not the Pope's theology for the universal church as his intrepid pastoral travels prove. We see him time and again raise up the crucified Jesus on his pastoral staff as if saying to the multi-millions before him and on TV, 'There is your Saviour and he is your future.' He strikes me as a man driven by the zeal of Christ: 'I have come to light a fire on the earth. How I wish the blaze were ignited!' (Lk 12:49) This Pope knows that the remnant mentality is not the dominant nor the preferred Christian mentality. The harvest mentality is. The harvest mentality is the call for world evangelisation and we find it in the 'great commission' that the risen Jesus gave to his apostles.

What is the great commission? It comes at the end of the Lord's earthly life and at the beginning of the Spirit's new life in the church. Clearly, it is a command and a hope, a theology and a mentality that is supposed to dominate the life of the church from the ascension of our Lord into heaven until he comes again in glory at the end of time. It is the very opposite of the remnant mentality and the remnant theology. It is full of energy, life and promise. It foresees vast numbers coming into the fold of Jesus; not just a faithful few remaining there. Here is Matthew's version of the great commission to the church:

> Now the eleven went to Galilee, to the mountain to which Jesus had directed them. When they saw him, they worshipped him; but some doubted. And Jesus came to them and said to them, 'All authority in heaven and on earth has been given to me. Go therefore and make disciples of all the nations, baptising them in the name of the Father and of the Son and of the Holy Spirit, and teaching them to obey everything that I have commanded you. And remember, I am with you always, to the end of the age.' (Mt 28:16-20)

So, I have no doubt at all that the church has a future. The Lord guarantees it. The kind of future it will have is mainly in the hands of the bishops because real power and decision-making in the Catholic Church rests with them.

Various people in the church draw up profiles (i.e. projections) of what the church of the future will look like.[20] Contrary to the predictions of doom, they actually foresee a numerically increasing church even in the western countries. But it will be, they say, a smaller church as a percentage of the general population.

They foresee large numbers of people retaining an attachment, rather than a commitment, to the church. This is due to a combination of reasons. Some of the reasons we have already met. Others are: pressure of work, time and family considerations; the transfer of volunteerism and energy from traditional church organisations to international help organisations and to the new personal and social health concerns; the sense that many people have that religion is not a blessing as we were taught but rather a major world problematic; the public's acceptance as values for themselves and their children of those goods the church frowns on as creature comforts; the attraction of alternative religious philosophies especially those that speak to the heart and that are holistic; the personal responsibility for decision-making that people's education has taught them and the consequent diminution of the church's guidance; the inability of the church to articulate its theology to them and the inability of its 'dry' spirituality to touch them emotionally; the Catholic Church's reduction of Jesus' saving message and the Christian way of life to such questionable priorities as having to go to Mass every Sunday under penalty, not using contraceptives, and being against abortion.

Much of the profiling of the future church contains assumptions, or hopes, that I feel are unrealistic. The profiles invariably think that there will be a lessening of the influence of Rome and the bishops over the church and a lessening of the institutional model of Church. They dismiss the pyramidal structure that we know and say that it will be replaced by sharing; they point to the failings of the intellectual tradition in theology and favour a mystical one that appeals to the emotions.

I said that I feel much of this profiling is unrealistic. Not undesirable, just unrealistic. I say this because Vatican II was in some matters the continuation of Vatican I. Between them, these two councils have asserted the centrality and power of the Pope and bishops in the scheme of things to a degree that modifies all profiles and models and serene projections; that contributes to the pastoral distancing that the bishops ironically complain about; and that depresses the people whether they are into lay consultation, the religious education of their children, co-responsibility for the church, or a self-determining faith and spirituality. At any rate, a consequence of Vatican I and II in combination is that the institutional and pyramidal model of church is stronger than it ever was and I suspect that no amount of hopeful profiling will change that.

As I wrote in another chapter, Vatican II appears to speak out of several theologies and appears to promote several models of church. I think it wants to make everyone happy. But at the end of the day its theology is one of disconnection. It is that combination of the Council's something-for-everyone and disconnection-on-the ground that has generated the often conflicting visions people have of their church and of their place in it. So much wasted energy and so much working at cross purposes have marked the years since the end of the council. So many hopes and so many profiles have come to grief already. That is why I am hesitant about seeing the actual future of the church in the more elaborate profiles of the church's futurologists.

There are a few aspects of the church's future that seem fairly predictable to me and that are commonly suggested by the futurologists in the professional theological community. As I suggested before, the kind of church we have in the years ahead will depend to a great degree on the vision and quality and energy of the parish clergy and on their relationship with their people. I say this for two reasons. First, because seminary formation – the emphasis on priests – remains one of the top concerns of Rome and the bishops. It fits their institutional model of the church as well. I say this secondly because it is the local clergy who most influence the people at the local level – not official theology, or the Pope or the bishop, or sins and scandals somewhere else. It is the 'men in the trenches' that matter most when all is said and done.

The kind of future church we will have will be more of a servant church than the triumphalistic one we have known to our grief. Ireland is becoming more and more a secular clone and a multicultural society. It may never quite become another Britain or America but the Irish church may well become a much more compassionate church and a moderating leaven in this new multicultural society. It will speak gently and not carry a big stick. In that way, the church will be more Christlike and true to its mission.

The continuance of the faith will depend in great measure on adult religious education and formation. As I've said and written nearly all of my life, the church consistently fails to educate its people in their faith to the level of their adult intelligence and to a degree that approximates to their secular sophistication. No wonder so many people see life as real and religion as childish with no real connection between the two. Our long-lived child-centred catechesis will have to be equalled by adult and inter-generational education.

So, for me, the church has a future. It will not be the dominant force it has been in the past. It will not be the power-broker and the politician that it has been. It has moved from being a triumphalistic church to a forcedly humbled one. Now it will progress from being a humbled church to a humble one. But it will not be just a shadow of its former self, a remnant church living out of a remnant theology. Smaller but committed congregations will ease their members more dependently, more supportively and more lovingly into each other's arms. The church internally, in the parishes, will be more communitarian and Christlike. That is an attraction for growth.

The future church will be a serving church, a servant of the poor especially. The future church will be a caring church, its resources pledged to the marginalised. It will attract many converts because people will see in the church the Christ that they are able to recognise instinctively. It will be a religiously educated and reflective church with an articulated faith for an educated age.

It will be a prophetic church. Ironically, its guidance will be freely sought by civil agencies and think tanks and social structures as society's interplay of rights, responsibilities, obligations, technologies and human concerns become more detailed and intricate from an ethical point-of-view. It will be a church that puts its past reductionism of God, of spirituality and of the gospel agenda behind it to embrace the whole Christ and the full gospel, and in their proper priorities.

It will be a church very changed from the one we grew up in. And even though it will be smaller and still have its lacks and its tensions and the inevitable weaknesses of its pilgrim humanity, the hope is that anyone belonging to it will feel spiritually at home.

This is a projection and a hope. I think it is up to the generation that asked most of the questions in this book, the ones I call the pivotal generation, to make it happen. Perhaps, surprised by grace, they will.

Bibliography

William J. Bausch, *The Parish of the Next Millennium* (Mystic, CT: 23rd Publications, 1997)

Catechism of the Catholic Church, (Dublin: Veritas, 1995 ed.)

Henry Chadwick, *The Early Church* (London: Penguin Books, 1993)

Rev Peter Connolly, 'Theology and the University: Literature and Theology,' *Irish Theological Quarterly,* XXXII, 1965

Donal Dorr, 'Sexual Abuse and Spiritual Abuse,' *The Furrow,* October 2000

Will and Ariel Durant, *The Lessons of History* (New York: Simon & Schuster, 1968)

James L. Empereur SJ, *Spiritual Direction and the Gay Person,* (London: Geoffrey Chapman, 1998)

Cornelius Ernst, ed., *Theological Dictionary,* (New York: Seabury Press, 1967)

Family Co-ordinator, (Washington: 28/1, 1979)

Louis Fischer, *The Essential Gandhi,* (New York: Vintage Books, 1983)

Austin Flannery OP, ed., *Vatican Council II,* (Dublin: Dominican Publications, 1996)

Brian Friel, *Philadelphia: Here I Come!* (London: Faber & Faber, 1965)

Sean O'Faolain, *The Irish,* (London: Penguin, 1969)

Joseph K. Pollard, *Medical, Moral & Pastoral Issues Today* (New York: Costello Publishing Co., 1980)

Pope John Paul II, *Crossing the Threshold of Hope* (New York: Alfred A. Knopf, 1994)

—, *Novo Incipiente Nostro,* Rome, 1979

—, Address to US Bishops, Rome, 1983

—, *The Dignity of Woman,* Rome, 1988

—, *Pastores Dabo Vobis,* Rome, 1992
Pope Paul VI, *Evangelii Nuntiandi,* Rome, 1975
Synod of Bishops, *Ultimis Temporibus,* 1967
The Oxford History of Ireland, ed. R. F. Foster (Oxford: University Press, 1992)
Alan Titley, *A Pocket History of Gaelic Culture* (Dublin: O'Brien Press, 2000)

Notes

1. James L. Empereur SJ, *Spiritual Direction and the Gay Person* (London: Geoffrey Chapman, 1998), p. 3
2. *Catechism of the Catholic Church* (Dublin: Veritas, 1995), pp. 285-6
3. Alan Titley, *A Pocket History of Gaelic Culture* (Dublin: O'Brien Press, 2000), p. 9
4. *Catechism of the Catholic Church,* p. 236
5. Will and Ariel Durant, *The Lessons of History* (New York: Simon & Schuster, 1968), p. 81
6. Joseph De Maistre in Durant, op. cit., p. 51
7. *The Oxford History of Ireland,* ed. R. F. Foster (Oxford: University Press, 1992), p. 223
8. Rev. Peter Connolly, 'Theology and the University: Literature and Theology,' *Irish Theological Quarterly,* XXXII (1965), p. 44
9. Sean O'Faolain, *The Irish* (Middlesex: Penguin, 1969), p. 119

10 *Theological Dictionary,* ed. Cornelius Ernst OP (New York: The Seabury Press, 1967), p. 72

11. John Paul II, *Crossing the Threshold of Hope* (New York: Alfred A. Knopf, 1994), p. 6
12. Louis Fischer, *The Essential Gandhi* (New York; Vintage Books, 1983), pp. 310-11
13. ibid., p. 311
14. Joseph K. Pollard, *Medical, Moral and Pastoral Issues Today* (New York: Costello Publishing Co., 1980), p. 103
15. Durant, *The Lessons of History,* p. 51
16. Brian Friel, *Philadelphia, Here I Come!* (London: Faber & Faber, 1965), p. 96
17. Durant, op. cit, p. 95
18. ibid., p. 98
19. Henry Chadwick, *The Early Church* (London: Penguin Books, ed. 1993), pp. 9-31

20 A good example is William J. Bausch, *The Parish of the Next Millennium* (Mystic, CT: 23rd Publications, 1997)